Race Relations

PHILIP MASON

Race Relations

OXFORD UNIVERSITY PRESS
London   Oxford   New York
1970

Oxford University Press

OXFORD   LONDON   NEW YORK

GLASGOW   TORONTO   MELBOURNE   WELLINGTON

CAPE TOWN   SALISBURY   IBADAN   NAIROBI   DAR ES SALAAM   LUSAKA   ADDIS ABABA

BOMBAY   CALCUTTA   MADRAS   KARACHI   LAHORE   DACCA

KUALA LUMPUR   SINGAPORE   HONG KONG   TOKYO

PRINTED IN GREAT BRITAIN
BY BUTLER & TANNER LTD
FROME AND LONDON

Preface

THIS book, like others in this series, is intended as an introduction to a subject. But, since it is a comparatively new subject and distinctly controversial, there is no single approach with which all who are interested in it would agree. It draws on a number of academic disciplines and in Chapters 2, 3, and 4, I have tried to summarize, and insert in the framework of my own general argument, the views of specialists in highly technical subjects such as biology, psychology, and psychoanalysis. I should like to acknowledge the kindness and help I have received from J. S. Weiner, N. A. Barnicot, and G. Ainsworth Harrison, although they are in no way responsible for my attempts to express biological conclusions in laymen's language. I have also a great debt to Marie Jahoda and Henri Tajfel, to both of whom I should like to express my thanks.

The general argument is based on my understanding of the history and social anthropology of the areas discussed in Chapter 7; it has been expressed at greater length in my own book, *Patterns of Dominance*, which will be published shortly before the present work. I could not have attempted to venture into such an extensive field without guidance, and I have leaned heavily on the work of Dr. Julian Pitt-Rivers for Spanish-speaking America, Dr. David Lowenthal for the Caribbean, and Dr. David Maybury-Lewis for Brazil. Books by these authors are shortly to appear which (together with *Patterns of Dominance*) were made possible by a generous grant from the Ford Foundation. But, although the coverage is wide, it does not include the South Pacific (except New Zealand) nor East Asia and there is nothing in it about Russian expansion in Asia.

An alternative course for a book of this length would have been to summarize thought on race relations, that is, the writings over the past few centuries of those who have given attention to this matter. But in the first place, this has recently been admirably done by Professor Michael Banton in the course of his *Race Relations* and I cannot rival his knowledge. In the second, although this is indispensable information for a student of race relations, for the general reader it may not be the most stimulating introduction.

Finally, I am very grateful to A. Sivanandan, librarian of the Institute of Race Relations, for help with the references and reading lists.

Contents

1
Is Race Important?

At the head of this chapter stands the question: 'Is Race Important?' By this is meant, does it affect human behaviour? The answer can be expressed shortly, though we shall come back later to discuss it at length; there is no means by which the intelligence or behaviour of any given human being can be foretold from the fact that he belongs to a particular biological group. But what people *think* and *feel* about race affects behaviour very much indeed. In the richest and most powerful country in the world, fires have blazed, men and women have been clubbed, shot, knifed, and gassed because black people are caught in a net of bad housing, bad schools, unemployment, from which they cannot escape and which they feel passionately was built by white indifference and cruelty. Beliefs about race were used to justify sending six million Jews to gas-chambers; they were used to justify tearing millions of Africans from their homes and keeping them like animals, forbidden to marry, liable to be sold at auction like any other article of farm equipment. In South Africa, Rhodesia, and sixteen American States there are still laws forbidding marriage between people of different race; in South Africa, people of the race indigenous to the continent cannot vote or join trade unions, nor can they own land except in special areas which make up less than one-sixth of the country.

Such a list could be continued almost indefinitely. But it would not tell the whole tale of how beliefs about race affect our lives. Nuclear war would bring consequences so devastating that we hardly dare to think of them; half the world is underfed and the growth of population threatens a spreading area of starvation;

these immense problems cry out for effective international action. But international action is hampered at every turn by jealousies and fears about race. They arise from the present fact that the rich nations are on the whole what is called 'white' and the poor nations are not; further, many of the poor nations have been colonial territories and look at much of their past with resentment. These emotions colour votes in the Assembly of the United Nations, appointments and procedure in Committees, even the operation of specialized agencies such as the International Labour Office. Even the Supreme Court of Justice at The Hague is regarded with suspicion by many because in its judgement on South-West Africa, all the judges who gave their judgement in favour of South Africa, came from 'white' countries, including the President whose casting vote decided the issue.*

Nor is it only international affairs that are affected. Since 1964, race has played a part in British politics. It is a temptation to any politician to take a quick means to popularity by outbidding his rivals in stirring up animosity against a minority; Britain begins to show how hard this is to resist. In the United States, Negro voters have long been an important electoral element, civil rights and poverty vital electoral issues. What is not so generally understood is that American foreign policy, by the fact of Negro unrest, is at every turn made to seem hypocritical and self-contradictory. All over the world, the powerful nations bid against each other for trade with the less powerful and, in the course of their rivalry, paint pictures of their competitors as nests of racial intolerance.

For the individual, ideas about race can be one of the most

---

* This judgement by the International Court of Justice at The Hague ended six years of litigation. The plaintffs were Liberia and Ethiopia, the only African states which were independent before World War II and therefore members of the League of Nations. They sued on behalf of all African states who had become independent since World War II; they asked, among other pleas, for a declaration that South Africa was acting illegally in extending to South-West Africa the system of separate development or *apartheid*. They argued that South Africa was bound by the Covenant of the League of Nations to govern in the interest of the native inhabitants and that separate development was not in their interest. The Court held by 8 votes to 7 in 1962 that it had jurisdiction and therefore heard evidence on the merits of the case but in 1966, also by 8 to 7, it dismissed the suit on another, but similar, procedural point, namely that the applicants had no legal interest and therefore no standing in the case. The Chairman on the second occasion was an Australian judge.

fruitful causes of human misery. Poverty may be eliminated—but skin colour cannot. What can be changed is the way colour is regarded, and how differently it is regarded in different societies will be one of the main themes of this book. But the change is not made quickly or easily, and the fact that colour has been used as a badge for social identification is bound almost always to affect both the man who bears the badge and the man who allots it. Hitler made the Jews wear the yellow Star of David because other Germans could not identify them without it. By that act he did something to the Jews which was bound to change them; after that they could not enter into relations with other Germans without remembering that they were Jews. But the Germans too were changed by what they had done; a people who have marked a minority as a separate people to be despised and hated have opened the way to something which infects the whole of their national life.

But, it may be argued, although these ideas do influence economic and political affairs, although they do make individuals unhappy, they do not make a *subject*; they are incoherent and irrational—indeed largely an illusion. This can never be an academic discipline, as history is, nor is it a clear-cut subject for study, like the Napoleonic Wars or Chinese porcelain. This of course invites the question of what exactly is meant by a 'discipline'. What follows is a personal view; this is a new subject in Britain and in its study there is not yet an orthodoxy that would not be challenged by more heretics than it can muster supporters. One dictionary definition of 'discipline' in this sense is 'a branch of instruction'; if this is a sufficient definition, to say that a subject is not a 'discipline' is simply to say that it is not regularly or usually taught. The objection in that case would apply to any proposal to teach anything new. But clearly more than this is meant; perhaps it is felt that a 'discipline' is a branch of instruction united by one basic assumption, as history depends for its intellectual interest on the assumption that a series of events can be linked together into a chain of causation, each flowing from what went before. This is valid up to a point; the study of race relations is not dependent on one single assumption. It does depend on a series of assumptions, which are still being worked out but which seem to hold together and form a whole. Like history, this kind of study assumes that a given situation in a given society is the

result of historical causes; like sociology, it assumes that there will
be resemblances between the structure of one society and the
structure of another and that comparison between them can inform
the student about the causes of both; like social anthropology, it
assumes that human customs arise from what, at some stage, have
been felt as the *needs* of a society; like psycho-analysis, it assumes
that whatever social forces may be at work, their effect on a given
human being will be moulded and shaped by the structure of his
personality.

It is the essence of this argument that the study of race relations
overflows the boundaries of academic 'disciplines' as at present
taught in the schools and universities of the United States and
Britain. That is not to suggest that these 'branches of instruction'
are arbitrary and artificial; they are not. They are 'real', in the
sense that to some extent they are dictated by their subject-matter.
History does, as I have suggested, demand a certain approach to
time and causation but this is 'real' because it is imposed by the
nature of time. Social anthropology demands a way of looking at
society, but something in the nature of society in turn demands
this attitude. But though these divisions have a validity of their
own and a value as methods of instruction and as habits of thought,
the problems of modern man sprawl untidily across them.

Is the objection, then, simply that the study of race relations
calls for contributions from several of the established 'disciplines'
or methods of instruction? If so, the point should be accepted;
this is not a method of training the mind and, if that is the meaning
of 'discipline', it is not a 'discipline'. It is a field of study—a subject
of burning importance in the world we live in, susceptible to
attack by the human reason and—it will later be argued—open
to some remedial action by makers of policy. And while it is not a
'discipline', neither, in one sense of the word, is it 'academic'. It
is not a kind of knowledge to be acquired for its own sake but
with the practical aim of influencing policy.

This is not to decry learning for the sake of learning, nor to
set up purely utilitarian standards of what ought to be studied.
It is simply to suggest that the main motive for the study of this
subject is man's need to understand the causes of his own misery.
Nor is it to exclude theory; the methods of research which will be
suggested involve the formulation of hypotheses and detailed operations to test them; this demands a body of doctrine within which

the hypothesis can be linked and from which fruitful hypotheses will emerge. In both respects, it is like studying cancer; the object is to cure. Health and disease must both be studied; no hypothesis will be of value unless backed by a general knowledge of medicine and the contributory disciplines—physiology, bacteriology, and the like.

It is more than a century and a half since the new subject of 'political economy', later called economics, was discussed by Adam Smith. *The Wealth of Nations* was published in 1776; it was not till 1905 that the University of Cambridge made Economics a Tripos. But, long before it received this accolade, economics had influenced the policies of statesmen. It is a subject which studies man in one aspect only—as an acquisitive animal; it considers human behaviour in so far as it is governed by desire to possess; it is thus, to some extent, an abstraction from life—and perhaps this is one reason why it begins to be respectable. The study of race relations is concerned with the total behaviour of men when they find themselves in a certain situation—in contact with groups they regard as differentiated from themselves by descent and by some physical differences. Such contacts are made increasingly frequent by modern means of transport—and contact is not only physical; radio, film, and television are a form of contact too. The emotions which operate in a race riot in Chicago may be more complex than those which bring men to the Stock Exchange or the market, but that is surely no reason for not attempting to understand them. Greed may be more easily predictable in its workings than hatred, but it would be hard to say that either was more serious in its consequences than the other—and surely its difficulty should not deter us from a study that might be as fruitful.

The trend of this argument is not that race relations should be taught in schools nor even widely to undergraduates, but rather that there should be *some* opportunities for undergraduate study and much more encouragement for postgraduate work in universities. But it is also important that the subject should be studied privately, not in degree courses, but by anyone who exercises the rights of a citizen and is concerned about the society in which he lives and the direction in which it is moving. From this point of view, the fact that it will not fit neatly into academic pigeon-holes will to some seem both an attraction and a challenge; it is exciting to deal with phenomena so complex that any attempt at generalization involves a continual widening of horizons. What is true of Los Angeles may well need modification in Harlem—and the next stage is to bring into the picture successively Cape Town, Lima, Singapore, Port of Spain, and Kingston. It next becomes necessary to lengthen the time dimension and call in history, and then to consider what psychological insights can add to sociological.

Finally, to some this subject will bring knowledge of the self. It will reveal, to a white man, hidden assumptions of superiority, withdrawals and reservations, fears of what others think, fears of abandoning secure positions. To one who is not white it may also reveal the kind of ambivalent feelings of anger, envy, unwilling admiration, guilt, love, and hatred that he once felt—perhaps without naming them—for his father. To some, this knowledge of self, like the emotional controversy the subject arouses, will be an attraction; there can be little doubt that for fugitives from life these will be additional reasons for shunning it.

This preliminary chapter has been intended to suggest that relations between races constitute a subject of vital importance in human affairs, one of absorbing interest and of practical value. It is a subject concerned with *life*, as it is lived day to day, not with any abstraction from life of one element. The student who is to achieve anything must not forget that he is dealing with living people, nor be so carried away by emotion that he fails to distinguish between hypothesis and proved fact. If he starves his heart, he will at best be dry in his presentation of the facts, and may seriously underestimate the vigour of the emotions he is dealing with; if he loses his head, he may easily fail to recognize how far his unstated premises have carried him towards his conclusions. It will therefore be as well for the writer to state here his own basic assumptions.

The first is that the evolutionary processes which led to human existence were gradual and immensely slow, but not continuous; they display distinctly marked stages. Gas, mud, rock appeared in succession, but life began a new phase. Here too, plant, fish, bird, mammal are distinct in spite of intermediate forms such as sea-anemones, fish with lungs, and four-footed, warm-blooded creatures that lay eggs. But a third great phase began with consciousness of self, and here the methods of evolution changed. Mutation, followed by natural selection between the resulting different strains, had been the principal method of evolution in the plant and animal world; with the growth of consciousness in man, ability to live together in a community became the condition of survival. The first rudiments of mind—ability to construct weapons, to combine for hunting—operated within the old framework and enabled a more successful group to survive where its rivals did not. But, as human societies became more complex, as elaborate social structures were built up, a specifically human kind of intelligence came into play which was able to go far beyond this, to observe the stars and the movements of the planets, to paint and build, above all to convey thought, not merely from father to son by verbal instruction but from one man to millions unborn by thought stored in writing. This could only develop in organized communities of a fairly advanced kind; to live in such a community demanded a framework of ethics, some restraint about the grosser physical needs, respect for the family and property of others in the community. Thought and art cannot exist unless someone else grows the food; this demanded a code of behaviour which in most respects was at variance with that disregard for any wants but its own which characterizes a plant, a baby, a non-social animal.

It is not necessary for my argument here to go beyond this to the next stage, the higher development of an ethical code from a mere system of restraints into something positive. Personally, I believe that we here enter a realm in which there are certain absolute values of goodness and beauty, and so far I agree with Professor Julian Huxley, whose account of evolution in his Romanes Lecture (published under the title *Evolutionary Ethics*, 1943) is so illuminating. It is not necessary to agree on this; what is central to this book—and I believe to the understanding of racial jealousy and conflict—is that man is both an evolved animal and a social animal; that he is only truly a man if he lives in society; that from his animal past and his social present there emerges a conflict from which he is rarely free. Man carries the heritage of his past; he is born selfish, 'how otherwise than a plant sucketh he and clutcheth? how with his first life-breath he clarioneth for food! craving as the blind fledglings in a thrush's nest. . . .'[1] But to live he must curb his sucking and clutching, or his hand will be turned against every man and he will be banished from society, an outlaw. He is at conflict; he is not perfectible; a just society is never

[1] References, numbered consecutively throughout the book, are listed on pp. 168–170.

attained. But some societies are more unjust than others; societies can be improved and reformed. It is idle to suppose that man will behave like an angel if society is destroyed; he is much more likely to behave like a beast. It is equally idle to argue as though society did not consist of individuals who have some freedom of action or as though individuals were not the product of social forces, as though their behaviour was not influenced by diet and upbringing, by education, family background and language, by the religion, culture and ethics of the past. It follows from the conflict inherent in man and from the dual nature of human societies, each an entity composed of individuals, that every situation at any given moment is unique. We are unlikely to find laws, like those of physics, which appear to operate immutably and invariably until an Einstein adds a new dimension. But we may, as between one situation and another, find resemblances, which may amount to patterns and which will guide us in dealing with the situation that confronts us.

Let us now move on to consider in more detail the statement, with which we began, that no one can predict the behaviour or intelligence of a given human being simply from knowing his biological group.

2
The Physical Aspect

1 Species and Race

In everyday language and in literature, the word 'race' has been used with a great variety of meanings; there are several columns of examples in *Webster*'s or the *Shorter Oxford Dictionary*. People still sometimes announce with an air of discovery that we all belong to the human race. At the other extreme, as late as the thirties of this century, 'the race question' in South Africa was used of relations between English-speakers and Afrikaans-speakers; what we should now call 'race relations' was known as 'the native question'. Most uses of the word imply some community of descent, but not even this is invariable; the *Concise Oxford Dictionary* quotes 'the race of poets'. No one has any right to say that a word *shall* be confined to any one meaning out of several, but in this book we shall exclude links which are primarily concerned with language, culture, and nationality and confine the term to populations distinguished from other populations by several physical characteristics* which are hereditary and are usually found in association with each other. The word 'population' is chosen because it is neutral; it is simply an aggregate of individuals, not necessarily linked by common interests or a common organization. But 'group' does carry these implications.

This is the point at which to make a distinction of great importance. To biologists, 'race' has the meaning just indicated,

---

* I use the word 'characteristic' where a biologist would say 'character'. In ordinary speech, the word 'character' usually stands for a whole made up from a number of characteristics, and I see no reason for departing from ordinary usage in a book that is not for specialists.

which will be elaborated in the next few pages. But the word is also constantly used in a variety of senses, of which the essence is to refer to a group distinguished from other groups by believing itself to be different in its essential nature, in some way that cannot be changed. It would make for greater clarity if this kind of 'race' was always referred to in quotation marks, and I shall sometimes refer to it more specifically as Notional Race, as opposed to Biological Race. Sometimes the two coincide but by no means always.

There are considerable difficulties about any consistent use even of the idea of Biological Race. No definition has been found which is entirely satisfactory, and the phrase here chosen is not to be regarded as a definition; it is a working guide only. The difficulty arises because, of all animals, man is the most mobile and the most adaptable. No other species has so wide a distribution or has migrated so freely and mixed so frequently. This means that there are seldom clearcut boundaries between races, as one might expect to find between populations which had been isolated from all contact with other populations over very long periods. American Indians and Australian aborigines were isolated before the coming of Europeans, but on the great land masses of Europe, Asia, and Africa there has been continual movement and mixture. Before proceeding with this point it will, however, be necessary to say something about the principles of taxonomy and about what is meant by a species.

Taxonomy is the branch of knowledge concerned with the methods by which plants and animals are classified. In its earliest days, it was hampered by a literal interpretation of the description of Creation in the book of Genesis. Linnaeus, who was to this subject what Newton was to physics, said: 'There are just so many species as forms were created in the beginning.' He was here influenced by Plato, Aristotle, and Thomas Aquinas as well as by Genesis. Plato had believed—and the other two had been influenced by his belief—that the specimens of any kind of thing which he saw—cat, dog, man—were imperfect copies of an idea or form which existed eternally. Linnaeus was looking for a unit from which systems of classification could be built, like a house from toy bricks. He made the species his unit and grouped species together to form the genus; tiger, panther, cat were species but were linked together in the genus *Felis*, though the *genus* was merely a convenience of classification. The species was something fixed and 'given'. Below the species was a sub-division sometimes described as a sub-species or, less precisely, a race. This was applied to distinguish a population which had been isolated from the main body of the species long enough to develop some differences. I spent some years in a Himalayan district where panthers caused much loss and danger to the inhabitants. They were as a rule bigger than the panthers of the plains, heavier in body, longer and darker in the coat. They might just have been called a different race. But they were certainly not a different species. The British shrew is a different colour from the continental variety and is classified as a distinct sub-species.

After Darwin, the species lost some of its taxonomic prestige. No one could say any longer that it had been instantaneously created in the beginning according to a pattern or form laid up in Heaven; in reaction, there was a tendency to think of the species as rather more of a taxonomic convenience, a man-made distinction. Clearly also it had become necessary to introduce a time element. *Eohippus* cannot be regarded as falling into the same category as its modern descendant the horse; one species can develop into another. This in itself implies a gradation, a shading-off, an absence of clear-cut lines. In the Eleventh Edition of the *Encyclopædia Britannica,* there is a long definition of the species by Philip Chalmers Mitchell, which begins with these words: 'A species is a grade or rank in classification assigned by systematists to an assemblage of organic forms which they judge to be more closely interrelated by common descent than they are related to forms judged to be outside the species . . .' This suggests that the classification depends on a *degree* of common descent, as judged by the systematist; it makes the species a man-made concept. But the tide has swung back; Dobzhansky in 1951 wrote: 'Though we cannot strictly define the species . . . the distinction is not merely a matter of degree.' In 1960, Dr. N. A. Barnicot wrote: 'The members of a species share certain features, which are presumed to be inherited, which distinguish them clearly from other species, and interbreeding leading to the production of intermediate forms does not occur in nature.' Here we have something which, if not a scientific definition holding good invariably, does provide an excellent working guide, to which there are three elements: several inherited features are shared—and this holds good of the race as well as the species; but also there is a *clear* distinction from other species; and fertile interbreeding does not occur in nature. Neither of these two latter points applies to local differentiations of the same species, which will interbreed when they meet, and which will then produce a variety of intermediate forms.

The importance of this for man now becomes clear. Man is one species; he shares many inherited features with other men and every kind of man is much more like a man than he is like any other species; he breeds with all other kinds of men and produces offspring who are fertile. The races of man are local variations; the differences between them are considerable—and we shall later discuss them—but they are not of such a nature as to provide absolutely sharp boundaries.

It is true that a typical West African looks very different from a typical Scandinavian, but there is no infallible demarcation for either group. The Bantu-speaking tribes who cover a wide area east and south from the forest areas of central West Africa share the typical Negro characteristics of the West African in varying degrees, but some also share characteristics with North African Berbers, Arabs, and Europeans. Again, the Scandinavian resembles typical specimens of the northern European people, and differences increase as one moves farther south, but they form a continuum of gradual change to Spain and into North Africa.

It is not in accordance with the facts either to pretend that physical differences do not exist or to suppose that they mark any population off so distinctly that classification can be free from doubtful cases. There is, indeed, a small school of physical anthropologists who believe that, because of past movements and mixing, the term 'race' is meaningless in respect of human beings and should not be used. But a majority would agree that, though the term is imprecise and should be used with great caution, it is the only term available for distinguishable populations which are not sufficiently well-defined to be classed as sub-species. What cannot be done is to make a scheme comparable to the organization of an army, with a neat subordination of each unit under some wider formation.

There are three major divisions of human population in the world—but not one of them is clearly defined, nor can they be named without some confusion. 'Caucasian' and 'white' are both unsatisfactory terms; this division of mankind must include people from the Eastern Mediterranean and Northern India who are markedly different in appearance from Scandinavians. The term Mongolian also covers a wide range of physical types. 'Negro', as already suggested, has two quite distinct meanings, being sometimes confined to the 'true' Negroes of the West Coast of Africa, and sometimes used much more widely to include the Bantu-speaking peoples of Central and South Africa and Caribbean and American populations whose ancestry includes many who are not African.

But the three major divisions are not only imprecise; they exclude large populations. The American Indians indeed are nearer to the Mongolians than to anyone else and might doubtfully be grouped with that division. But in Africa the Bushmen, Hottentots, and Pygmies can hardly be put under the head Negro, nor can the Melanesians of the Pacific, who resemble them. There are Veddoid peoples of South India who do not fit easily into the scheme; there are the Australian aborigines, whom some scholars would class as 'archaic whites'. Complex affinities and resemblances can be traced but the only points about which one can be dogmatic are negative; there is no 'pure' race and it is hard to know what the term means; there are no hard and fast lines of division without exceptions and border-line cases. On the other hand, there is no smooth gradation permitting one to arrange populations in an ascending and descending scale in respect of one characteristic which would not produce a broken scale in respect of another characteristic; for example, skin colour would produce one scale, height another.

We must now be rather more precise about the nature of human differences.

2 Differences in Man

The differences between the various races, strains, and local variations of man are of two main kinds. It will be convenient to call them quantitative and qualitative; these are not the scientific names but this is not a book for specialists. By quantitative differences are meant those in respect of which there is a continuous range within each of the populations we are comparing; they may also be called multifactorial because a very large number of genes combined to produce the effects which are visible.

An obvious example is height. Here, and in all these quantitative differences, we compare the *averages* of populations, and there is overlapping. If we say that Englishmen are taller than Japanese, we mean that the English average is greater than the Japanese average; the tallest Japanese will be well above the English average. In a comparison of different populations, the most extreme were both from Africa; tallest were the Nilotic Dinka and shortest the Pygmies of the Congo. The Dinka averaged over six feet, the Pygmies four feet nine inches. But the tallest Pygmies were the same height as the shortest Dinka.

It is worth spending a little longer on height as an example of a quantitative or multifactorial difference. It is easy to see and to measure and, to some extent, it can be used to illustrate more important characteristics. There is a considerable hereditary element in height; in technical language, 'the heritability index is around 0·80'. What this means, in simplified and untechnical language, is that four-fifths of the difference between one individual's height and another's is likely to be due to genetic factors and one-fifth to environment. But this is a matter of averages; if environment is markedly different, for example if one man has been starved and another fed on good quality high-protein food from birth, the genetic potential will not be realized in one case, while it will be in the other; of the actual difference in height, at a given moment between two individuals, more than 20 per cent of the difference may be due to environment. The genes of two men might be such that with exactly equal environment one would have been five feet five inches and the other five feet nine inches; that difference would then be 100 per cent due to heredity. But if the short man is underfed and the tall man well-fed the difference might be between five feet three inches and five feet eleven inches —a very marked difference, of which 50 per cent was due to environment. It is also important to remember that in' every individual there is a store of concealed genes; the phenotype—the sample of humanity we see—is, in effect, an average combination of the many genes provided by the two parents. Let me quote from J. A. Fraser Roberts:

Let us consider a metrical character [e.g., height] determined by a series of genes Aa, Bb, Cc, and so forth, the alleles denoted by capital letters making for larger measurements and those by small letters for smaller measurements. In a randomly breeding population very few individuals will have all, or nearly all, the large letter genes or all the small letter genes. Most persons will have a mixture of both.[2]

It is by 'unscrambling these genes' and releasing a hidden store of potential variation that the breeders of domestic animals and plants have produced such startling changes in average size and yield in so few generations; the average yield of eggs per hen in England, for example, has doubled in twenty years and during the eighteenth century the average weight of sheep or cattle sold at Smithfield doubled. Even when this improved potential is brought to the surface by selective breeding, a good environment is still needed to achieve the high yield. Note also that the breeder of domestic animals has not only the power to mate high performers with high performers, but he knows exactly what he is trying to obtain. In a room of any twenty to thirty people, Dr. Fraser Roberts continues, 'the genes are there which would permit the development of a strain with an average height of six feet eight inches or alternatively of four feet ten inches'. But so long as man is a wild and not a domesticated species, that is unlikely to happen.

It would be contrary to the facts, however, to assume that in a 'wild' or free population the hereditary elements in height are 'fixed' for individuals except for a slight range of difference due to good food and other environmental factors, and that the averaging-out of random mating will therefore fix the average height of the population permanently. As is well known, mediaeval suits of armour show that even the better fed classes of the period were well below the average of the present; more dramatic have been the increases in height reported from Japan between 1940 and 1970.[3] It is clear, therefore, that an improved environment and free mating can bring to light some of the hidden potential.

Height can stand as a good example of the kind of difference that is quantitative and can be measured and of which the inherited element is carried by a number of genes. The important points for our purpose are, first, that although averages of this kind of characteristic vary between one population and another, the distribution within each population is such that there is an overlap; secondly, that there are potential reserves in the pool of genes of any population which, in suitable circumstances, could be developed so that strains would appear that were distinguishable from the original stock.

Height appears to be a simple characteristic and not much

loaded with emotional content; there is no sensible reason for being ashamed of being short. Yet in this brief discussion, there has been a slight implication, difficult to avoid and here consciously not avoided, that it is better to be tall—and it is legitimate to ask why. Is being tall really an advantage? Within what limits and for what purpose? And are there not different aspects of tallness, even for the limited purpose of athletics? Long legs are an advantage to a sprinter or boxer but not to a swimmer or an oarsman; height may be due to a long back as well as long legs; a weight-lifter or shot-putter needs a different figure again. And height again may stand as an illustration of the way we think about qualities in other people. Tell an Englishman that the English are generally taller than the Japanese and he will feel slightly complacent; tell him that the Dinka are generally taller than the English and he will reflect that height is a characteristic of very little importance.

The second kind of distinguishing characteristic, which we will call qualitative, is usually carried by a single pair of alleles (or alternative genes) or by a small number of pairs, so that an individual either has, or has not, the characteristics; he cannot have it more or less. The perfect example is the system of blood-groups known as A, B, AB or O; everyone must have one or the other of these. They are distributed among the populations of the world in different proportions; most populations have among them all the three genes by which these four blood-groups are inherited. The exception may be the Amerindians, who, at any rate South of Panama, may once have all been O. It is impossible to be sure, because a good deal of mixture had occurred before anything was known of blood-groups. In general, the B type is more frequent in Eastern Europe than in Western, more common in Asia than in Europe, very rare among Australian aborigines. But only the frequencies with which they occur differ between races; if an Englishman of group B required a blood-transfusion, there would be serious consequences if he was given blood of group A from another Englishman, but not (other things being equal) if he had blood from a Chinese of group B—and the odds on a Chinese having it would be greater. The frequency of these groups in a population may tell us something of its history; for example, blood-groups have revealed surprising affinity between Icelanders and Scottish, Welsh and Irish populations; what had been expected was that they would resemble Scandinavian. But one series of blood-groups cannot tell us much about the racial affinities of an individual. On the other hand, there are now many known systems of blood-groups in addition to the first system of four, and as each is identified, the likelihood is narrowed, until the investigator can say with a high degree of likelihood whether a drop of blood comes from a West African or an Englishman. He arrives at this through the conjunction of a number of factors of the qualitative kind, but no single one is, by itself, a factor sufficient to distinguish an individual by race.

Of the two kinds of difference we have been looking at, then, the first, or quantitative, will give a difference of *averages* between two populations; but the individuals who make up the populations are likely to overlap in their measurements, the individuals at the top of the measurement scale in the lower group scoring more than those at the bottom of the scale in the higher group. The other kind of difference, absolute or qualitative as regards the individual, is, between populations, a matter of the *frequencies* with which the form occurs. Let us now turn to consider to what extent these differences are of any practical importance.

3 The Practical Effects of Difference

The point of making these distinctions about the nature of racial difference is to make it easier to consider whether there is any reasonable justification for regarding one race as 'better' than another and therefore as entitled to any kind of preferential treatment. It is essential to be frank about this and to make perfectly explicit the kind of beliefs that are held and the consequences that would follow. We are not at present discussing the argument that might is right and justice the interest of the stronger, which was put forward by Thrasymachus in Plato's *Republic* more than two thousand years ago, and had of course been the practice long before that. But many who would, at least in public and consciously, repudiate such an argument have a feeling they are not always willing to formulate, that certain races are 'better' than others and that it is a waste of time and money to try to help those who seem backward. It is often argued from this unspoken assumption that 'they' must wait till they have reached 'our' standards before they enjoy certain benefits, or alternatively, that some special kind of education or religion or housing is suitable for 'them' but not for 'us'.

Such arguments may be put forward as an excuse, conscious or unconscious, for maintaining a state of affairs favourable to the speaker, in which case they are only a cover for the argument of Thrasymachus. Yet this, as I have said, the speaker would often explicitly deny, concealing from himself the consequences which follow from his assumptions about inherent superiority. These continue to be expressed in a variety of forms. They lie, for example, behind the view sometimes expressed that the presence in Britain of the children of immigrants will constitute 'a terrible danger' to our national life. More subtly, in the *Harvard Educational Review*, Winter 1969, Professor Arthur Jensen argues that a different kind of education ought to be provided for those who find difficulty in using abstract concepts but who can learn more easily by association, of which one form is simply learning by heart. Among these would be reckoned a high percentage of those 'of low socio-economic status', a category which, needless to say, includes a large number of Negroes, who have been selected by the social system for the bottom of the ladder because of their low IQ, which is largely hereditary. His argument specifically states that a cleavage on class lines is being widened by the American and Western European system of education and of selection for lucrative and interesting work. He suggests a 'greater flexibility' in education which, by separating those judged capable of conceptual thinking from the others, would surely increase and perpetuate this cleavage. He lays, if anything, rather more emphasis on the hereditary element in class differences than in race differences, but here we begin to see how similar are the problems arising from these two systems of distinguishing one group of people from another. We shall return to this argument and others of the same kind in the next chapter, but for the moment we must confine ourselves to the general principle. The assumptions and consequences in the background have to be brought to the light, and the first question to be asked is: What is meant by 'better'? Better for what?

Here we must go back to Chapter 1 and the points made there about evolution. In an earlier stage of evolution, it was possible to regard survival as the justification for a species, and a somewhat similar criterion is adopted by geneticists when they consider a new hybrid form. They ask if it is 'viable'. Will it live in its environment? Again, the breeder of domestic animals and plants knows what he wants—eggs from a hen, milk from a cow, high yield from wheat, from all three resistance to disease. But, as we have said, this is not enough for man; among specifically human achievements are ability to live in a society, to create beautiful objects, and to create a society which gives satisfaction to its members.

But, on this criterion, can we not simply judge that peoples who have not yet achieved high civilizations have failed? Just as the species which cannot survive in its environment must give way to one that can, so—it may be argued—we must judge that those which have created no stable societies, no enduring monuments, must be judged inferior. This argument contains one doubtful assumption and one fallacy. First, it makes an arbitrary judgement about the actual achievements of a 'civilized' compared with a 'primitive' society, but as a rule with a very slight knowledge of what one of the two is like. Can we be sure that a tribal existence before contact with industrialized peoples was less satisfying, less truly human, than city life today? Can we really be sure that tribal life *had* achieved as little as we think? It is irrelevant to say that people leave the tribe for the city when they can, because, apart from the fact that some do not leave, the tribe has changed as soon as it is in contact with industrialized people. There *was* satisfaction in hand craftsmanship and a fixed network of relationships and obligations which is now destroyed. As to the artistic value of works by people at a fairly primitive stage of organization, tastes change and today high prices are paid for objects which our grandfathers would have regarded as no more than curios. Nonetheless, I believe we must judge that most people will prefer living in an industrialized society to a tribal, even if the satisfaction provided by the former soon comes to seem hollow.

The fallacy, however, seems inescapable. It is that one can judge the future from the past. But—to take one example—there was a point in time when Athens was a small town whose King had authority in an area about ten miles across and thirty miles long, and had achieved nothing. Two centuries later, the people of this small area had still done no more than create a unified state the size of an English county; they would be utterly forgotten if it were not for their startling—indeed unsurpassed—achievement in the two centuries that followed. In this period they built a city rich in temples of such beauty that they are still remembered, still visited; they produced poets, dramatists, and sculptors whose works still move people, philosophers whose influence is still powerful and whose thought for two thousand years has been at the heart of Western civilization. The Incas, again, were an obscure mountain tribe, who, in less than two centuries, established a classical empire, exceptionally well-ruled, two thousand miles long, through some of the most difficult country in the world, with roads, aqueducts, irrigation channels, a system of storing grain against famine, an elaborate network of taxation, and rapid imperial mails. Rome was civilized when Britain was barbarous, and Cicero advised a friend to buy no British slaves because they were too stupid and backward to learn anything. To an Egyptian of the sixth century B.C. Rome would have seemed a small and barbarous Italian town still forced to capture its women from its enemies, the Sabines. The wheel turned and by the time of Julius Caesar, Rome was 'civilized', 'developed', a strong military power to which Egypt was a decadent colonial appanage. In our own century, Russia, under the last Tsar, was an underdeveloped, hardly industrialized, country.

It is not, then, an acceptable idea that, because a people have not achieved anything yet, they will not achieve something in the next century. Men have used fire and made tools for perhaps half-a-million years; the frontier is constantly being pushed back by fresh discoveries but it is clear that, whatever the period during which our predecessors can be called human, it is tiny in relation to geological time and the evolution of life, on the other hand immense in relation to recorded history. And in recorded history, the ups and down of peoples are startling; who are we—the British and Americans—to despise the Chinese, whose ancestors discovered gunpowder and made exquisite porcelain while ours wore woad?

There is a further point, generally neglected, which is of considerable importance. Surely it would only be extreme degrees of difference that would provide any rational grounds for differential treatment of different races of men? To justify a system such as the South African, under which men of one race are forbidden by law to do certain jobs, it would surely need to be shown that *all* men of population A were, in some respect that was of importance for modern life, measurably inferior to all men of population B; or on the other hand, that one population was of a different species, not breeding with the other? But no one today alleges that either of these degrees of difference in fact exists. In all measurable differences there is an overlap, and as we shall see, the advantages are not all on one side; nor is there the kind of difference that can be classified as that of a species.

Nonetheless, people have tried to find differences that would justify classifying other human beings as quite different from themselves and thus justify keeping them in slavery or subjection. There is nothing new about this. Aristotle was exercised by the fact that the civilization he knew was based on slavery. Slavery was not then associated with Africa, rather mainly with north-eastern Europe, and the problem did not present itself as primarily one of race or descent, although our words Slav and slave are derived from the same word. But it was, perhaps, all the more clearly a moral problem. Slaves did not behave like free men; they must therefore be slaves by nature, Aristotle concluded. It is a modern thought that by making them slaves, their masters force them to behave as slaves. Similar motives, a similar unease, were strong in the nineteenth century. The French Revolution had proclaimed liberty and equality as the creed of one great state. In the other powerful states of Europe, men were anything but free or equal; in the United States and Brazil, a large part of the population were held as slaves, and in a form of slavery more degrading than that which Aristotle had contemplated. It seemed necessary to justify both the European and the American forms of subjection, and writers were found to meet the need.

The controversy about species had been active throughout the eighteenth century and had been considerably influenced by a theological doctrine which goes back to St. Thomas Aquinas and, through him, to St. Augustine. Why should a good and loving God create slugs and snakes? Because—came the answer, expressed of course with far greater subtlety than here—without them the world would have been incomplete; something that might have existed would have failed to be, and there would have been a gap. This, sometimes called the Principle of Plenitude, implied a continuous spectrum, the Great Chain of Being, and led many naturalists before Darwin to question the idea of fixed species and to favour explanations of nature which suggested a continuum. It was therefore satisfactory to suppose that there was some kind of continuum from the 'higher' races of man through the 'lower' to the great primates. 'Missing links' were sought; and 'as late as 1831 [writes Banton in *Race Relations*] it was possible to publish respectably a multi-volume work in which orang-outangs and chimpanzees were classified as human and set in a regular hierarchy along with the other races of men'. And Edward Long, the historian of Jamaica, believed in 1774 that 'an orang-outang husband would not be any dishonour to a Hottentot female'.

By the middle of the nineteenth century, there had been a considerable development and such ideas were no longer respectable in quite that form. But there was a spate of racialist writing. In France, de Gobineau produced a complicated theory of the decline of civilizations about which perhaps the most important part is what was remembered. 'A society is great and brilliant only as far as it preserves the blood of the noble group that created it, provided that this group itself belongs to the most illustrious branch of our species.' To this the corollary is that: 'the white race originally possessed the monopoly of beauty, intelligence and strength. By its union with other varieties, hybrids were created, which were beautiful without strength, strong without intelligence or, if intelligent, both weak and ugly.[4] The arguments used by de Gobineau and his followers contributed to the attempted extermination of the Jews. They led also to many intellectual absurdities; the nobility in France were of a different 'race' from the commons; blond, Teutonic, long-headed people were bold and adventurous—natural rulers—while dark, round-headed people were timid and submissive. Here it becomes apparent that de Gobineau and his followers are no longer talking about Biological Race. They have switched to Notional Race; this applies to most of the writing about 'race' in Europe which burgeoned in the last century—about Celts and Teutons, Latin 'races' and the like.

Meanwhile, the assertion continued to be made that Negroes were hardly human at all. In 1863, in the first presidential address to the Anthropological Society of London, Dr. James Hunt maintained that 'there is a far greater difference between the negro and the European than between the gorilla and the chimpanzee', and that 'the analogies are far greater between the negro and the ape than between the European and the ape'. This led him to such conclusions as: 'the negro becomes more humanized when in his natural subordination to the European than under any other circumstances' and 'the negro race can only be humanized and civilized by Europeans'.[5] It is tempting to digress as to what he meant by 'natural'—the subordination was still fairly recent—but the temptation must be resisted. What must be insisted on is the long period during which intelligent men were, usually without awareness of their motives, trying to find justification for the subjection and domination of one part of mankind by another. Here a generalization begins to emerge; the aristocrats, the dominant group, insist that differences between them and their subordinates are natural or permanent; once he begins to think about it, the subordinate insists that they are accidental. To this development of thought from the subordinate side, we shall return; here it is important to be aware of this background to the physical enquiries that were conducted.

Darwin himself was careful to avoid most of the conclusions in support of which his name was invoked. But his discoveries did not interrupt the tradition of thought that sought to differentiate man from man; the semi-popular social philosopher, Herbert Spencer wrote of the 'survival of the fittest'—it was not Darwin's phrase— and helped to encourage the idea that the processes of nature which had, as their culmination, produced Man—and above all Western Victorian Man—had achieved this by ruthless competition; the species had been perfected by the elimination of the weaker and it was right, natural, and fitting that the same process should continue between peoples. Karl Pearson carried the doctrine to its extreme; 'the theory of the state became biological'. Not individuals but whole tribes, nations, races were slaves by nature in a new sense, not merely by natural constitution, as Aristotle had thought, but by the inexorable laws of nature as revealed by Science. Such ideas quickly spread to more popular writers and to the common speech of the time and there is, for example, a story of Kipling's which speaks of a man 'obeying the old race-instinct which recognizes a drop of White blood as far as it can be diluted'. It is an interesting phrase, for a number of reasons; how, one wonders, had this 'old race instinct' been implanted in the people of India? Not, surely, by natural selection and the processes of evolution; it was little more than a century since the few English in India had been suppliants to the Moghul Emperor, holding their few scattered factories at his pleasure. And why was it that in America the almost exactly opposite belief was held by people of English stock, namely that one drop of Negro blood, 'so far as it can be diluted', made a Negro? But, however illogical, such things were constantly said, and to many it seemed that the circumstances of the time lent support to them.

There was every incentive, then, to find hard, incontrovertible, physical facts that would differentiate man from man. Clearly, the size of the brain has some importance for the specifically human functions; the great prehistoric reptiles had a tiny brain-case in relation to the size of their bodies, and have ceased to cumber the earth. Man's cranial capacity is usually between 1250 and 1550 cubic centimetres, while a gorilla—with three times the body-weight—seldom has more than 600 c.c. Could it be then, that members of the lordly white master race had brain-cases larger than those of the non-whites? It would seem once again necessary to show that *all* white men had larger skulls than all non-whites if popular ideas about race were to be sustained; it would also seem to suggest that among white people the man with the biggest head was most to be admired. Nobody ventured to make either of these assertions. Undeterred, however, by such considerations, industrious craniologists made many collections of skulls and measured their capacity. But the results defied generalization on racial lines. All human brains were found to lie within a range of between 1100 c.c. at the smallest end of the scale and 1800 c.c. at the largest; averages, by ethnic groups, showed Europeans fairly low in the scale. In one collection of measurements, the Europeans averaged 1450 c.c. and were beaten by several Asian groups, two Eskimo tribes, one American Indian, and Maoris, Tahitians, and Africans. In another collection, Javanese scored 1595 c.c. against 1478 c.c. for a collection of Scottish skulls. It is perhaps even more convincing that palaeolithic skulls found in Australia and South Africa— though they constitute a very small sample—seem to be larger than those of most modern men, while one Neanderthal skull is 1620 c.c.

These are comparisons of empty skulls. The exact capacity of a live skull cannot be judged in the same way, but the head-measurements of 4,500 boys and girls of twelve years old and over 1,000 undergraduates were found to show no direct positive correlation with their academic achievement. In other experiments, a very slight correlation was found between absolute brain weight and achievement, but none between achievement and ratio of brain weight to body weight. This result may therefore suggest no more than that the better nourished do better at school. And finally, the ratio of brain to body weight, which in man is about 1 : 35, is almost the same in gibbons, while for some small South American monkeys it is 1 : 15. To sum up, it seems clear that, while intelligence cannot develop if the ratio of brain weight to body weight is very high, as in the brontosaurus, within a certain range of ratios there is no direct relation between size and quality.

This particular argument is quite out of date, but there are still English people who vaguely believe they have read or heard that Negroes are less intelligent than white people because they have smaller heads. Again, it was found that in apes the fontanelle, the open space in the skull of the new born, closed relatively earlier than in white men, and it was stated—without proof—that this was so with Negroes, whose brain therefore could not develop so quickly. This however has been shown to be without any foundation whatever. But perhaps there was a difference in the brain itself; it was suggested that the thickness of the cortex or outer covering was significant and very small samples suggested that there might be a difference between Africans and Europeans. But the racial difference has not been sustained, nor have various theories about the convolutions of the brain, which might provide a greater total external surface, nor the relations of the various parts to each other. There are considerable differences in both respects between individuals but such racial differences as exist cannot be related to intelligence.

Then, perhaps, the shape of the skull was important. Skulls were classified as dolichocephalic if the breadth was less than 75 per cent of the length, brachycephalic if more than 80 per cent, mesocephalic in between. The Nordic type was tall and long-headed and it was argued that leadership and adventurous qualities went with the long skull. But the theory fell into disrepute as it came to light that while South Germans tended to have short skulls many African populations had long, and indeed the most characteristic African skulls are long. But though banished to the scientific attic, the theory lingers on among those to whom these ideas are convenient.

'Purity of the race' is another widespread idea which needs discussion but it comes best in the next section, on the mixture of races. There is a group of hypotheses which have been tested by scientists and to all of which the answer is similar. They all derive

B

from the idea that although skeletal differences might not be significant to the extent hoped for, there might be differences in reaction to environment which had a racial basis. The glands might function differently or the rates of metabolism—the conversion of food and air into heat and energy—or the rates of response to a stimulus, or the onset of puberty—all these have been explored and show great variety between individuals and links with a habit of life, but not a racial pattern that can be dissociated from environment. Ephedrine is circulated through the body in greater volume at times of emotional stress and the working of the glands concerned with this function will therefore be more lively in a man whose way of life involves stress, personal antagonism or success in persuading people to agree with him—in a politican or a salesman—than in a man who spends long hours monotonously planting cabbages. But between the averages of black men and white men leading the same kind of life, there is no detectable difference. The same kind of conclusion has been reached about metabolism and response to stimuli. The onset of puberty is widely believed in Britain to be earlier in hot countries and it is true that cold, hard exercise and simple food delay the beginning of menstruation. But the evidence is against the idea that sexual maturity is earlier among 'primitive' peoples.

Another belief still widespread among white people is that Africans—or in a still cruder form, 'coloured people'—are biologically 'more primitive' and 'nearer to the ape' than themselves. This of course is connected with the old idea of the Great Chain of Being. It may mean that in the process of evolution there was a split at an early stage, one branch then developing more rapidly than the other, or it may mean simply that the Negro shares more characteristics with the ape than white men do. Neither idea is true. It is not always possible to determine the 'race' of ancient skeletons, because obviously skin colour and hair form perish, but in general it seems likely that of the three main divisions, the Negro branch was the most recently differentiated from the main stock, the Mongolian and the 'white' having separated earlier, and the most ancient stocks having characteristics that are predominantly 'white'. But it is hard to see that the point has much significance; a strain that was differentiated comparatively recently might prove to be a biological improvement or the reverse.

The question of characteristics shared with the ape has more relevance. But in fact characteristics which can be called ape-like are fairly evenly distributed among the major races. Body hair is the most obvious; Mongolian and Negro strains have markedly less than 'whites'; the Negro form of hair is quite remote from the ape's. Apes have no lips and in this respect the Mongolians are most like them and the Negroes least. The ear of the Negro is said to be evolutionally more advanced than the 'white' man's; in teeth, chin and lower jaw the reverse is the case, but the 'whites' are more likely to have some trace of the heavy ridge above the eyes that we think of as primitive in gorillas and in reconstructions of Neanderthal man. Dr. Hooton has stated the point succinctly: 'No physical anthropologists can rank the existing races of man within an evolutionary hierarchy in the order of their distances of departure from the anthropoid apes, because each race shows its own combination of anthropoidal, primitive human and advanced specialized characters.'[6]

It is also believed that some differences exist between races in respect of liability to disease, and of course it is true that there are great differences in the incidence of diseases and to some extent in immunity. Any population—whether of plants, animals, or human beings—is particularly susceptible to any disease to which it has not been previously exposed and to which it has therefore developed no immunity. The arrival of Europeans had disastrous results for Tahitians and American Indians; on the other hand, Europeans in West Africa appeared far more vulnerable to malaria and yellow fever than the inhabitants. In general, it seems that the human body can produce the antibody necessary to combat any disease to which it is introduced; American Indians are not now killed by measles nor does a doctor inoculating for yellow fever use a different serum for an Englishman, a Negro, or a Chinese. There is more tuberculosis in Ireland than in England but this is less likely to be due to any difference in genetic make-up than to poor food and dark, wet huts in Ireland in the last century and to energetic health measures in England.

Disease, then, is usually conveyed by infection from one individual to another and, in general, proneness or immunity are a matter of the past history of the individual, his exposure to bacteria or viruses which produce an appropriate antibody, and the resistance resulting from general good health, sunlight and protective foods. But this is a generalization to be treated with some care.

There are two well-known exceptions and there may be more. One exception is the connexion between malaria, anaemia, and what is called the sickle-cell trait, a genetic characteristic which causes the red blood-cells in certain circumstances to congeal in shapes which, under the microscope, sometimes look like a sickle. This characteristic is found in Africa, more rarely in parts of the Mediterranean basin and South India; a person who carries the gene for this trait from one parent only seems to be immune to some of the more dangerous forms of malaria. But if both parents carry this gene, their child will suffer from anaemia and is likely to die in childhood. In some African populations, this trait is present in about 40 per cent of the population.

There is also the danger of haemolytic disease of the new-born for the second child of a Rhesus-negative woman married to a Rhesus-positive man. In Britain five persons out of six are Rhesus-positive; the proportion of Rhesus-negative in some other populations is considerably higher. But the danger is still one for *individuals* whose blood-systems are incompatible and this may be the case if both are British. There may be other connexions between blood-groups and liability to disease of which little is known.

To sum up, differences between human individuals in skill, aptitude, training, experience are considerable; so are the physical differences of build and stamina. The difference between the *average* of one strain or recognizable descent-group and another are much less. Provided they have had some opportunity for acclimatization, human groups from all over the world respond to heat, cold, exercise, altitude and nutritional variations with remarkable similarity. There is a modern trend to see these similarities in physiological adaptations to circumstances as minimizing the external differences on which emphasis was formerly placed. In respect of all the qualities for which one human being is chosen rather than another—for a team of athletes, for a job, for a mate, for a neighbour, for a friend—there are many questions which it is sensible to ask, but they are questions about the individual—his education, his blood-group, experience, achievement. To know his race will not give the answer to any of these questions; at best, it can suggest that a person of one race is more likely to possess a certain characteristic. As J. A. Fraser Roberts has put it:

the usual differences [from the point of view of classification] are still those which are striking or identifiable but essentially of minor consequence to survival and well-being ... The striking characteristics that distinguish races are the marks of people who have successfully adapted themselves to particular environments ... these are multifactorial, continuous, overlapping, the bit of the iceberg above the surface. In fact, the things that races share in common are much more important than the things that divide them.[7]

4 Genetic Mixture

Questions about genetic mixture are constantly raised in popular discussion about race, and often phrased in highly emotional terms. To see the matter clearly, it is necessary to make a distinction between the biological and social consequences; this is necessarily somewhat artificial because for man there is no way of rearing children which is not affected by the social system. Training at home and education, self-confidence, opportunity for success— these will make all the difference to a man's behaviour. Where the social system is such that the hybrid is denied advantages of this kind, people of his father's group and his mother's may alike condemn him. And it will very often suit them to regard his failure as due to biological causes.

In the case of man, the crossing of distinct strains or races has been regarded in very different lights in different societies, and even at different times within the same society. The conqueror of Mexico, Cortes, had a son by an Indian lady of noble blood, Malinche (known after baptism as Doña Marina), who acted as his secretary and interpreter and was of great value to the Spanish; this son was made a Marquis of Spain and even a member of the exclusive Order of Santiago. He was to all intents Spanish, his illegitimacy and his mixed blood condoned by the sovereign. On the other hand, many an Indian woman bore a child of a Spanish father who was brought up as an Indian, the union being acknowledged and perhaps forced upon her. Parellel cases of both kinds occurred in the early days of the British in India, but later there developed in India a self-contained society of mixed European and Indian descent; they were once knows as Eurasians and later as Anglo-Indians and were kept socially at a distance alike by the British and by high caste Indians, while they in turn kept themselves at a distance from Indians of the lower castes. In the British colonies of America and in South Africa the whites excluded those of mixed blood from their society and in South Africa there was no place for them in tribal African society. We shall deal later with these very varied social reactions at more length, but it is necessary to make the point that it is rare for people who are biologically hybrids between two strains to grow up in an atmosphere in which they are not subject to some social stress. The *social* effect of their position has often been deplorable. The one example always quoted of what biologists call complete panmixis —absolutely random mating—which was also completely free from social disapproval was that of the mutineers from the Bounty who fled to Pitcairn Island with an equal number of Tahitian women. There was no one else there, so they were all one society.

But let us, so far as we can, consider what are likely to be the purely physical consequences of genetic mixture. Unfortunately, anyone who tries to consider this dispassionately and accurately is at some disadvantage in dealing with reckless and emotional statement, because the proper caution of scientists forbids them to be dogmatic on the subject, and that for two reasons. First, man is a wild species (as the biologists say) with whom, in this field, it is not possible to make large-scale experiments with control groups. And, as a corollary to that, it is not possible to make any firm projections from hybridization in one species to any other. What we know of plants and animals may suggest a probable hypothesis but it cannot provide a rule. What is stated accurately must therefore sound hesitant. But practical conclusions can be firm.

To understand the difficulty of making a forecast, we must remind ourselves of the two main kinds of difference in man which we have already discussed, the quantitative, multifactorial, measurable difference conveyed by a number of genes, and the qualitative difference conveyed by one gene or pair of genes— something which a man has or has not. The nature of heredity was for long concealed by the fact that the obvious differences are quantitative, and heredity was therefore thought of as something liquid, like blood, rather than something discontinuous, like marbles, which is nearer the truth. But Mendel's discoveries, when at last they became known, showed the working of heredity in respect to the kind of difference conveyed by one gene. He experimented with peas of two strains, a normal and a dwarf; the gene carrying the characteristic of normal height is dominant, that for the dwarf height is recessive and the two are alternatives. If peas of the two strains are bred together, the offspring will have one gene from each parent, one normal and one dwarf, but since the normal is dominant, they will be of normal height, the recessive dwarf element going into hiding. If D is the normal and d the dwarf gene, the original parents, from the two separate strains, will have genes which may be shown as DD for one strain and dd for the other, each with the same gene from both parents. The first generation of hybrids will get one gene from each parent and will all have genes Dd, but only D will show, because d is recessive. But if these hybrids mate together, in sufficient numbers for an average to be struck that evens out chance variations, the likelihood is that one quarter of the resulting population will be DD, one quarter dd, and one half Dd, of which only D will show. So the practical—and, until it is explained, puzzling—result is that in the parents' generation one set of parents are normal and an equal number dwarf; in the first hybrid generation all will appear to be normal, though all carry one recessive gene; in the third generation, three-quarters will appear normal and one quarter dwarf. But of the three quarters who appear normal, two will carry the recessive gene.

This is just how the distribution of blood-groups A and O would work out in man, because blood-group A is dominant over blood-group O. But of course it is absurd to imagine a Pitcairn Island with the sexes equally balanced and carefully selected for this one qualitative characteristic carried by a single gene. In any actual mixing of populations, far more characteristics will be involved, operating in different ways. There are some single alternative genes of which neither is dominant; if red shorthorn cattle are crossed with white, the second generation will be roan, having red and white hairs mixed to make an intermediate type, while in the third generation, one-quarter will be red, one-quarter white, and half roan. Once the Mendelian principles are known, and once it is known that a characteristic is carried by a single allele or pair of alternative genes, and whether either of the pair are dominant, the results of a cross in respect of one qualitative characteristic, such as a blood-group, can be foretold. But, as we have seen, for most characteristics which are visible and can be measured, many genes are involved; for these quantitative characteristics, such as height, forecasts cannot be made with certainty even for a pair of individuals from the same strain, because both the parents are in fact averages of a large number of factors. Their children are likely, but not certain, to be intermediate between the parents and, if mating was completely random, there would be a continual tendency away from extremes and back towards the average height of the population.

If we consider two distinguishable strains of wild plant or animal, within a species and therefore able to mate successfully, we must assume that the differences have fitted each of the two for its own environment. Therefore, any hybrid population which is intermediate is likely, if it finds itself in either environment, to be better suited than one of the parents, less suited than the other. But this is not certain; it may not be able to survive in either; it may appear virtually as fit as either parent strain in either environment. The crossing of two strains may, and often does, produce in the first generation *heterosis* or hybrid vigour; the children of the Pitcairn islanders from the Bounty were taller than the average of their parents. But this hybrid vigour is not always maintained in later generations.

Purely biological conclusions cannot therefore be reached from the free behaviour of man. But hypotheses may be deduced from experiments with domestic animals and plants, or from experiments in laboratories. In the former case, breeding, as we have said, is aimed at specific results—more eggs, wool or meat, a lower intake of food, whatever it may be—in a specific environment. The method is an alternation of cross-breeding and in-breeding combined with culling, that is the rigorous rejection of all but the best. The modern race-horse for instance was produced by crossing Arab and other Eastern strains with European breeds and then breeding to the best that resulted. The enormous increase of the last twenty years in the production of eggs per head of poultry in relation to food has been produced by crossing established breeds, generally White Leghorns and Rhode Island Reds, in various proportions, sometimes breeding in to the hybrid strain thus produced, and sometimes continuing with first-crosses. Here, where it is clear what is wanted and when both breeding and environment can be controlled, there is absolutely no doubt that judicious crossing can be beneficial. But it does involve the rejection of crosses that do not turn out well.

In the laboratory, geneticists tend to use species whose generations succeed each other rapidly; fruit-flies and mice have been favourites. Survival in an environment has usually been the test by which a cross is judged to be successful and, as already stated, scientists are extremely reluctant to predict whether a cross will be successful until it has been tried. What does seem to be a tendency is for random breeding within a fairly homogeneous population to produce, in respect of quantitative characteristics, a closer cluster of intermediate types round the middle point of the population's range. On the other hand, if this population is crossed with another, there may, in respect of this same quantitative characteristic, be an increase in the number of exceptional individuals at either end of the scale. There is some likelihood, but no certainty, of a general increase of vigour—hybrid vigour or heterosis—but, if so, it will not always be sustained in later generations.

Obviously these lessons cannot be exactly applied to man so long as he is, in any sense of the word, free. We can control neither mating nor environments and we should not be prepared to reject the unfit. But it seems reasonable to suppose that on the whole the same tendencies hold good. We know that in a small static population which has been closely isolated for a long period inbreeding does often produce physically harmful effects. Human history has been a record of migrations and conquests and of subsequent mixing. It is to be expected that this would sometimes lead to hybrid vigour and to the production of unusual people with a combination of exceptional qualities. One could point, for instance, to the sixteenth century in Spanish history, during which the New World was discovered, conquered, and colonized and Spain became the most powerful nation in Europe; one could suggest that this was due to the previous five centuries of Arab and Moorish occupation, which had added to the already very mixed genetic stock contributed by Romans, Visigoths, and Iberians. But it would be a hazardous argument and quite inconclusive; other good reasons could be adduced for Spanish success and other successful periods in other countries where the genetic addition was more remote. There is also some confusion in the Spanish example between the state and the individual; there were Spaniards in this period who displayed almost incredible energy but it would need to be proved that they were in fact of recently mixed blood and in fact the presumption is generally that they

were not. There is a stronger argument for *cultural* hybridization
than for biological.

It is a more legitimate point that all strains of man have been
mixed so continuously and for so long that there is no such thing
as a 'pure' race, and that the least mixed seem on the whole to
have been least successful. But it is not very clear what a 'pure race'
means. If it means 'isolated from contact with others for long
periods', it applies to few groups indeed; in Asia, Europe, and
Africa mixture has been constant. The Amerindian people are
generally thought to have been isolated from the rest of the human
species for some 25,000 years, but they show differences between
their own groups and appear to have come into the continent from
the North at different periods and subsequently to have mixed.
The Australian aborigines have also been isolated for a long time
but have not been a very progressive people. If on the other hand,
a 'pure race' means an aristocracy who have succeeded in keeping
themselves aloof from a conquered people for a long time, this has
been more frequent in mythology than fact, but, when it has
occurred, has usually had serious social effects to which we shall
return.

But we may conclude with some confidence that, if man had been
isolated in small groups for long periods without mixture, 'the
broad evolutionary potential' of each group would have been restricted. 'There can be little doubt that the reticulate nature of
human evolution has greatly facilitated man's biological success.'[8]
We do not know enough to predict with any certainty dire disaster
as the result of mixing two populations; the purely biological
arguments seem to be slightly in its favour. As between two individuals, of course, the considerations are quite different but the one
point that must be made—whether we look at the biological, social
or psychological consequences—is that marriage *is* between
individuals and it is about the results for individuals that they
should think.

3
Intelligence

---

1 Innate and Acquired Intelligence

WE have discussed the physical characteristics which distinguish
the different strains of mankind and it is clear from what has so
far emerged that there is no reason to suppose that any of these
physical characteristics will be the *cause* of any difference in intelligence. But one of them might still be the invariable accompaniment of a difference in intelligence that was of importance for
mankind, the sign by which it could be recognized.

Whatever we mean by 'intelligence'—and this is one of the main
points for discussion in this chapter—on certain points we can
be dogmatic from the start. 'Intelligence' is a quantitative not a
qualitative characteristic; it is carried by a great many genes, not
by one, and like other characteristics of this kind, such as height,
there is an overlap between any two populations that can be validly
compared. Both will display a typical distribution, with most
members scoring something near the average of the population,
while both above and below the average there are scores which
get fewer as they get higher or lower. The top scores of the lower
population will be well above the average of the higher. We can
also be dogmatic on a second point, that both heredity and environment contribute to 'intelligence', still using the term in this broad
and as yet undetermined sense. What part is played by each is one
of the points we have to discuss, and it has to be considered step
by step, each step at the same time illuminating the nature of the
'intelligence' we are trying to analyse or define.

Most people, as soon as they pause to consider it, will perceive
a distinction between 'native wit', something with which each

person is more or less endowed, and his mental capacity as a mature adult; we recognize that this capacity can be improved by education and stretched by continual endeavour, or allowed to lie undeveloped. The point is made by the courtier who introduces Bottom's play in *Midsummer Night's Dream*. The actors, he says, are: 'Hard-handed men that work in Athens here/That never labour'd in their minds till now / And now have toiled their unbreath'd memories / With this same play. . . .' It will be convenient if from the beginning we label 'native wit' Intelligence A; it is the genetic endowment, the potential, the ground-plan, the architect's sketch on which a building will be based. Intelligence B is the intelligence achieved by the mature man; it is the building at any given moment—never quite finished till death—in which builders as well as architect have played a part.*

Early in this century determined attempts were made by educational psychologists to isolate Intelligence A. Intelligence tests were devised which were meant to show not what a child *had* learnt but what he *could* learn. The Binet–Simon Metrical Test, devised in 1905, was meant to grade children in school in a continuous scale ranging from (in American terms) 'very bright' to 'very dull'. This test was later improved and the Stanford Binet Intelligence Scale is now generally regarded as the standard for the measurement of intelligence. It is to this that reference is usually made when Intelligence Quotient (IQ) is given a numerical value.

Tests of this kind were first used on a massive scale in the American Army in 1917–18, when nearly two million recruits were classified by test scores and grouped by country of origin. The results gave a distinct advantage to people of British and north-west European origin; southern and eastern Europeans came next, American Negroes last. At first, these results were thought to show differences in the innate intelligence (Intelligence A) of the original stock. But reflection suggested that the samples came from immigrant stocks of very different kinds; the first British colonists in America, for example, were many of them in protest against the social, political, and religious system and were probably above the national average in originality and initiative, while the South Italians, Russians, and Poles were often of peasant stock and had

---

* The terms Intelligence A and Intelligence B were first used by the Canadian neurologist D. O. Hebb.

been driven from home by poverty. And the first group had a considerable start of two or three extra centuries in more favourable conditions. More certainly, knowledge of the English language was a significant factor in the results. Finally, the results were very much what would have been expected if the recruits had been graded according to what in Europe would be called class, but in a classless society is called Socio-Economic Status (SES).

This line of thought was further explored; the further experiments went, the more difficult became the task of devising a culture-free test. Language was the first difficulty; the vocabulary of a white American middle-class home was usually much larger than that used in a family of Southern Negroes, where schools were segregated and opportunities for white-collar jobs almost non-existent. The questions sometimes contained words the person questioned had never heard before. But more subtle was the difference of approach and the nature of the concepts on which the question was based. Klineberg has an admirable illustration of this. A white child from one of the remote, mountainous parts of the South—areas whose people were known as 'hill-billies' and used to be caricatured in *The New Yorker* and *Esquire*—was asked: 'If you had ten cents and spent six on candy in the store, how many would you have left?' The child pondered and replied that he had never had as much as ten cents and he did not know how he would spend it if he had. But it would certainly not be on candy, which was not sold at the store; it was something mother made at home. This was clearly an intelligent child, who assumed that he was being asked a practical question; he addressed himself to solving it as an actual situation. A child with a different background would immediately perceive that the question came from the abstract area of mental activity know as 'arithmetic'. I recall just the same difficulty with an African chief under the British system of 'indirect rule' in the fifties; I wanted to know what was his order of priority among the needs of the people for whose administration he was responsible. As he had little formal education, I tried to avoid words like priority and asked what he would choose if an American millionaire said he might have a million dollars to spend on the people of his district. He treated the question in the same way as the hill-billy boy; no American millionaire ever did come to his district but if he did, and if he made such an offer, the chief would think it essential to know what he wanted in return and would go to consult the District Commissioner. It took a long time to find out that he had a clear idea of priorities and put education before hospitals or roads.

If words and concepts are soaked in cultural background, perhaps pictures might be free; much thought was once given to devising tests based on drawing or on perceiving the mistakes in drawings that were supplied. But the difficulties were not much less; an early example was a drawing of 'a house' with a door, four windows, and a gable roof—a convention familiar in the kindergartens of the period—but no chimney. The children were asked what was missing. A Sicilian boy supplied a crucifix instead of a chimney—but an Eskimo accustomed only to igloos or a Zulu to round huts would have been wholly at a loss; so indeed would a child brought up among many-storied blocks of flats who had not met this convention. Two groups of children in the United States, one white, one Indian, were each asked to draw a horse and a man; they were not marked for artistic skill but for what they put in and left out. On the horse, the white group scored around 70 per cent of the Indian; on the man, the proportion was reversed.

It would be tedious to go over all this forgotten ground; the result of a life-time spent on this subject was sadly recorded by Otto Klineberg: 'The history of mental testing of ethnic or racial groups may almost be described as a progressive disillusionment with tests as measures of native ability and a gradually increasing realization of the many complex environmental factors which enter into the result . . .'[9] 'We would do better to admit,' writes Professor Vernon, Professor of Educational Psychology in the Institute of Education, London University, many years later, 'first that we do not know whether there are [statistically distinguishable racial] differences in Intelligence A and are unlikely to be able to find out; secondly, that it is really Intelligence B that concerns us and this is best regarded as the level of development of those intellectual capacities which a particular culture favours.'[10]

2 Intelligence as a Response

The impossibility of comparing the intelligence of people from completely different backgrounds was admirably and at length exposed by Biesheuvel in his book: *African Intelligence*. But—to condense and simplify—the point becomes at once apparent if one takes extreme examples. Let us choose a Bushman from the Kalahari desert who is still leading the simple food-gathering life of his ancestors and is uncontaminated by contact with Europeans. Not many such are left, but until recently there were a few. Such a man's intelligence has been concentrated on food and water; he knows where to find water in the desert and where to find watermelons which will assuage thirst; he knows how to store water in ostrich-shells under the sand. He knows the movement of antelopes, how to snare birds, various lore about what berries may be eaten. He can find his way in the desert but he would be completely lost if set down in the middle of London. Similarly, a man brought up in the heart of London would be absolutely ignorant of all that the Bushman had learnt in the course of his life. He would die in the desert unless the Bushman helped him. The *content* of what they had learnt would be so utterly different that it would be impossible to devise any means of comparing the *ability* of these two to learn. Even in respect of memory, an important element in all learning, they could not easily be compared; show one of these two a collection of twenty objects and his ability to recall and recite the twenty will largely depend on the associations they carry for him, on whether they have any meaning.

But we are interested in a good deal more than the content of what has been learnt, rather in ability to learn. And here we begin to approach more closely the question of what we mean by 'intelligence'. There is a serious danger of circular reasoning at this point; it is permissible to say that intelligence is what intelligence tests measure, but we must then be careful to remember that by saying this we have defined nothing and still need to ask what intelligence tests are about. In a recent, and highly controversial essay in the *Harvard Educational Review*, Winter 1969, Professor Arthur Jensen remarks that intelligence, like electricity, is easier to measure than to define. Later in the same essay, he emphasizes that the term should be reserved for the 'rather specific meaning I have assigned to it, namely, the general factor common to standard tests of intelligence'. It is not, he says, completely synonymous with mental ability, but is 'a capacity for abstract reasoning and problem solving'. It is 'important in our society mainly because of the nature of our traditional system of formal education and the occupational structure with which it is co-ordinated'. Thus its importance is derived 'from societal demands'. And, in the same general sense, he quotes with approval O. D. Duncan who says: ' "intelligence" is a socially defined quality . . . a correlation between IQ and occupational achievement was more or less built into IQ tests . . . what we now *mean* by intelligence is something like the probability of acceptable performance (given the opportunity) in occupations varying in social status. . . .' Take this with Vernon's point, already quoted, that Intelligence B is 'the level of development of those intellectual capacities which a particular culture favours . . .' and we begin to see some light. The whole question has been further greatly clarified in Professor Vernon's recent book *Intelligence and Cultural Environment*. Here he distinguishes the 'intelligence' measured by intelligence tests as Intelligence C. It is this that Professor Jensen is discussing.

This distinction further underlines the point already made that the Bushman's intelligence cannot be compared with the Cockney's; society has made different demands on them. To elaborate, we have no means of discovering Intelligence A—the genetic endowment—of any man. Intelligence B is the result of the challenge an environment sets to Intelligence A, the genetic endowment. In this extreme case, the challenge is so different that comparison cannot be made and any estimate made of Intelligence C would be meaningless. But this extreme example, though useful for the argument, is unlikely to arise in practice. When we come to more practical comparisons, such as those constantly made between American whites and Negroes, this point about the social definition of intelligence and its relation to probable performance becomes vividly enlightening; still more illuminating is O. D. Duncan's parenthesis about opportunity in the quotation above. 'Intelligence C' is what Western society requires of those who are to achieve high status, worth-while occupations, success, and acclaim. The point is stressed by Jensen over and over again. But if a person belongs to a minority group, most of whom feel that this kind of success is out of their reach, society is surely not making this demand upon him. It is of the first importance to understand that there is a double point here; he belongs to a minority group which has not achieved the kind of skills that bring success and therefore he will make a poor showing when 'they'—the successful —test his skills. But not only that; he does not see any prospect of achieving success and so has no incentive either to perform well in the test or to acquire the skills that would enable him to perform well.

What intelligence tests measure, then, is the response to a social system of a person with two qualifications; he is sufficiently a part of the social system to be equipped with its concepts and systems of thought and—even more important—he sees some advantage in responding to its demands. With this essential conclusion in mind, let us go on to consider the division between hereditary and environmental components of intelligence. But, first, it will not be wholly a digression to return to Professor Jensen's point that, in American and West European society, 'intelligence'—that is Intelligence C—does not mean the whole of 'mental ability'.

Intelligence-testing becomes increasingly subtle and varied. It measures as much as it can. But there are many dimensions of Intelligence B—man's intellectual response to his environment. Testing began in the Western culture, and with measuring the logico-mathematical ability to respond to standard Western education based on Greek, Latin, and mathematics. It is this kind of intelligence which makes aircraft and ensures that they arrive on time. In Western culture, which is increasingly becoming international, it is of the widest importance. But it is not the only area of human mental ability. Within this area, there is the rare and immensely important factor of originality. There is the mind which considers existing data, and proceeds from them to a hypothesis or synthesis. But the original mind gives the existing data a shake and turns them into a new set of data; he considers the whole complex situation from a new angle and perceives that the data presented to him are the wrong ones. It is not easy to be sure that a test will find such a mind's full ability.

There are two other dimensions of mental activity which are outside the logico-mathematical field. They are even harder to define than intelligence, but may be given the temporary labels of sensitivity and wisdom. A high degree of logico-mathematical intelligence often goes with a low degree of sensitivity—to beauty, to personal relationships, to the subtleties of social atmosphere, of shades of meaning. And the reverse is true; a person extremely sensitive in such matters is often ill at ease with Euclidean reasoning. And by wisdom is meant an often slow, often very imperfectly expressed, but apparently intuitive, understanding of the human factors involved in a situation and the lines on which they are likely to develop. The point was once expressed to me in a context highly relevant to race relations. An Afrikaner missionary was explaining to me his inability to sit at table over a cup of tea with Africans who were ordained ministers in his church. It would be the thin end of the wedge and he would not know where to draw the line with other people. Did he then regard them as inferior, I asked. Yes, he replied, they are inferior in education, but not in something for which he could supply only the Afrikaans word: *Lewenswetenskap,* the science of life, something in which they often had much to teach him. He meant what I mean by wisdom.

It is not a main strut of my argument to belittle Intelligence C, the 'intelligence' measured by intelligence tests; my intention is rather to emphasize the point admitted by Professor Jensen and, indeed, by almost all psychologists, that it is not the whole of mental ability. Indeed, this is something implicit in all our institutions. We do not automatically make the man with the highest IQ the Prime Minister or the President: we wait to see what other qualities he will develop. We judge him by Intelligence B, his total response to the situation in which he finds himself. Further, it is my purpose to avoid confusion; we must try not to hark back to any hope of isolating Intelligence A. It is even more important to accept the view that Intelligence C is the still imperfect formulation of a demand made by a society. To this follows the corollary that there is likely to be a poor response from those who are not part of the society, who are not equipped with its concepts and see no prospect of reward in responding to its demands.

3 Heredity and Environment

But does not this concept of Intelligence B as response to a social demand neglect the contribution of heredity to intelligence? The point has only a limited validity. Intelligence B has developed in response to an environment and a challenge: what heredity has contributed is Intelligence A. We have agreed that this cannot be isolated, but no sensible person would deny that it exists. Can we determine what proportion of Intelligence B has been enabled to develop by heredity or genetic endowment? There is in fact a better line of approach to this than through attempts at a culture-free test.

There is a valuable discussion by Dobzhansky of various observations made on twins, brought up separately and together.[11] He is a geneticist and will not be accused of trying to underrate the importance of heredity. But let us use he figures of Professor Jensen, which are more recent and more comprehensive; he will be the more convincing as a witness because I do not agree with all his conclusions. Here is a table, simplified from one of his, which shows: 'Correlations for Intellectual Ability'. (He has, I fear, forgotten that 'intelligence', in his 'rather specific' sense, is not the same as intellectual ability. He means Intelligence C.) The correlation would be complete if two monozygotic twins (that is, from one egg—what are commonly called identical twins) who were reared together performed exactly alike in all tests; this correlation would be represented as + 1·00. If no agreement is found beyond what is to be expected by pure chance, then the result would be expressed as $\pm$ 0·00. The table has been simplified by omitting some relationships such as second cousins, uncles, and aunts, and by omitting slightly different columns of values corrected for various theoretical reasons, which produce tidier results; the first value in my table becomes in the theoretically corrected result 0·00 and the last 1·00, while the correlation for brother and sister or for parent and child becomes 0.50. The less digested result seems to me more revealing. Dizygotic twins are twins from two eggs which happen to be fertilized simultaneously and are genetically no more related than any two siblings.

TABLE 1

Correlations for 'Intellectual Ability' [from Jensen: *Harvard Educational Review*, Vol. 39, No. 1]

Between Unrelated Persons:	
Children reared apart	−0·01
Foster Parent and Child	+0·20
Children reared together	+0·24
Between Collaterals:	
Siblings, reared apart	+0·47
Siblings, reared together	+0·55
Dizygotic Twins, different sex	+0·49
Dizygotic Twins, same sex	+0·56
Monozygotic Twins, reared apart	+0·75
Monozygotic Twins, reared together	+0·87
Between Parent and Child:	
Parent (as adult) and Child	+0·50

A glance at this table will reveal that the resemblance between foster-parents and unrelated foster-children is important; the correlation is 0·20, very like that between unrelated children reared together. This must surely represent environment. Compare this with the results for identical twins; the correlation is 0·75 when reared apart, 0·87 when together. For siblings—that is brothers and sisters—it is 0·47 and 0·55. A layman would be inclined to deduce from these figures that the contribution of heredity to what is here loosely called 'Intellectual Ability' is about four parts to one part for environment. Jensen, after some pages of statistical discussion, records with approval a finding by Burks of a 'heritability coefficient' of 0·81. Some years earlier, in a review of the evidence, expressed in less technical language for the benefit of scholars from other disciplines, Professor Vernon concluded that: 'the hereditary contribution to differences in measured intelligence is still vastly greater than the environmental factors, possibly in the ratio of four or more to one . . . the figures seem to me reasonable *provided that* one is concerned only with children within a fairly uniform culture.'[12] In fact, of course, all these experiments have proceeded on this basis and there are no cases recorded of two identical twins, one brought up in Chelsea and one by Australian aborigines. But with Professor Vernon's proviso, let us take it as settled that the ratio is something like four to one. In the last chapter, we noted that it was much the same for height.

What, in the light of this, are we to make of the consistently lower scores by Negroes than whites in the United States? Jensen, summarizing much evidence, says that they test on average about 15 points lower on IQ than whites; 'when gross socio-economic level is controlled, the average difference reduces to about 11 IQ points.' Now, before dealing with this in present-day terms, it is necessary to go back a little into controversy which is now obsolete.

4 Opportunity, Incentive, Response

Let us take as a turning-point the decision in 1954 of the Federal Supreme Court that 'separate but equal' was not 'equal'. It was a turning point in a sense not then understood; it seemed the culmination of a long period of liberal endeavour, but in fact it was the beginning of the end of liberal optimism. Until then, the assumption among white liberals, and also Negro intellectuals, had been that two processes were at work; Negroes, by leaving the South and moving into the industrial North, were raising their standard of living and, in desegregated schools, were getting a higher standard of education. They were thus becoming steadily more like white people in every respect. At the same time, the spread of education and tolerance among whites would gradually bring the majority to accept the minority in every walk of life. Opportunity and incentive would thus increase and there was a prospect of social mixing coupled with a steady reduction in differences in IQ.

In support of this general hypothesis, evidence was adduced of a rise in IQ in the case of Negroes who had left the segregated school system of the South and moved to schools in New York. It should here be added that, during the thirties, figures from the Southern States for expenditure per child at white and Negro schools varied between five and three times as much for whites as for Negroes. For both they were much lower than in the North. The children of recent Negro immigrants to New York seemed (in Klineberg's research) to pick up steadily; those born in New York appeared very close to white children of comparable Socio-Economic Status, and to do better than recent white immigrants from the South. These results led to a controversy as to whether emigrants from the South should not be presumed to have more initiative and ability than those who stayed behind; there was a contrary hypothesis that there would also be many who did not move because they were successful in the South. Klineberg found that the emigrant children who improved when they reached the North had not, before leaving the South, been noticeably brighter than their equals in age. This controversy has diminished in importance; it finds no place, for example, in the recent discussion in the *Harvard Educational Review* of Spring 1969.

This is largely because of the depressing developments in the North, the growth of 'ghettoes'—sections of the great industrial cities which are predominantly Negro, in which schools are not legally but in fact segregated, and from which the escape to white-collar employment and middle-class housing conditions is rare. Here the incentive to respond to the demands of society is slight indeed. The atmosphere has been brilliantly described by Claude Brown in his book *Manchild in the Promised Land*. This is far indeed from being a learned work of psychometrics but is important to an understanding of the social background to measurements of Intelligence C. Claude Brown describes the life he knew as a little boy on the streets in Harlem. He wanted to be someone who was admired and noticed. But the way to that was not going to school regularly, but playing hookey from school and stealing and fighting. 'If I hadn't fought or stolen I would have been just another kid in the street.' 'When the bigger guys started messing with you, you couldn't hit them or give them a black eye or a bloody nose. You had to get a bottle or a stick or a knife.'[13] Those were the first demands which the society he knew made on him; he soon progressed beyond such innocent forms of delinquency to far more sophisticated offences against the conventional moral system of the West.

That is why it is not enough to 'adjust for Socio-Economic Status'. To account for the performance of any group it is essential to consider its ambitions. The important question is, whose approval is sought; is it that of the other kids in the street? Claude Brown's father had come from the South and his ambition was to hold a steady job as a janitor or a liftman—an elevator attendant— and to keep out of trouble with 'the Man', which means white people in authority. This was not good enough for Claude and his generation but they saw no clear way to anything better. He was obviously an unusually gifted person but the only society he knew made demands on him which, to conventional society, are appallingly anti-social.

The year 1954 was suggested as a keypoint in the American scene; it was a moment when it seemed as though liberal optimism might be justified. But since then Negro despair and impatience have grown steadily. Negro incomes have on average not risen so fast as white and, since the number of Negro unemployed—and especially young unemployed—is much higher than of white, there is a growing gap between those Negroes who have been able to get into white-collar jobs and the rest. Jessie Bernard has written of 'two Negro cultures'[14] and two broad groups certainly can be distinguished, those who have some prospect of making good in white terms and those who feel they have no hope and who have accepted the demands of another society, which they feel to be their own. American Negroes test on average between 11 and 15 IQ points worse than whites in 'probability of acceptable performance'; about two-thirds of them *know* it is improbable that their performance will be accepted. Is this very surprising? Their 'environment' includes a lack of any incentive to respond to the challenge of the culture in which they find themselves.

In the light of this concept of intelligence as reaction to society's demand, some of the points formerly often made become of secondary significance. Testing has to take account of the reaction of the person questioned to the questions; if he regards the questioner as hostile or superior, he will not do well. There are groups, notably some American Indian tribes, who regard it as a breach of good manners to show knowledge of something of which another is ignorant. There are also isolated rural communities who have little understanding of relating a task to measured time; Hebridean islanders as well as American Indians have shown this trait.

To summarize, the majority of educational psychologists would back the propositions that Intelligence A cannot be isolated; that Intelligence B is a reaction to a given culture; that environment, which includes incentive, plays a part in determining Intelligence B, differences in which may on average be regarded as in the proportion of one part environment to four parts of heredity; that Intelligence C—that which is measured by Intelligence Tests—does not represent the total of mental ability. This means that no one can say with certainty that there is or is not an ineradicable difference between the averages of intelligence of any two racial groups; we simply do not know because we cannot isolate Intelligence A. We do, however, know that in the United States there is a difference as regards Intelligence C.

But, in considering this, it is essential to understand imaginatively the position of the Negro American and to perceive his lack of valid incentive to respond to the demands of American society. It is also necessary to take sufficient account of protein starvation, both prenatal and postnatal, and its effects on the brain and therefore on Intelligence B, not merely Intelligence C. It need hardly be said that protein starvation, usually accompanied by parasitic worms, is directly related to low Socio-Economic Status, that is to say to class as much as race, and that a disproportionate number of Negroes are in the lowest group in this sense. It must also not be forgotten that most black Americans have some white genes. Finally, it would be fatal to consider this difference without taking serious notice of any society but that of the United States and Britain.

A single incident will make the point; I have recorded it before, but in my own mind it clinched so many laborious trains of reasoning that I cannot omit it. I was in Barbados, in conversation with the headmaster of the high school, which has a good academic standard. The island had then a population about 93 per cent black, about 7 per cent white; the school however had about one-third white boys. I asked if there was any difference between black and white in academic performance. 'Oh, yes,' was the answer. 'We do now and then get a white boy who comes up to the black standard, but it is rare.' Was this due, I asked, to any deterioration of whites in the tropics? No such hypothesis, he answered, was required. The school had virtually every white boy in the island, while the others had to compete for places; almost every white boy had an assured job to go to, in an office or on a plantation, so they did not work so hard; finally, their fathers were usually in business or managing sugar plantations and so did not use books as tools to the extent that was common in black homes, where the fathers were civil servants, lawyers, or doctors. Academic performance, it is generally agreed, is more heavily influenced by environment than IQ; nonetheless, it is broadly true that where incentive, numerical proportions and background are reversed, so are the results.

4
Pressures from Within

1 The Group and the Self

PERHAPS the main point that has so far emerged from this discussion is the difficulty of defining Biological Race or of assigning hard and fast boundaries to any racial group. But there are also two broad generalizations. In the quantitative or measurable differences between man and man, such as height and intelligence, variations within groups are greater than variations between the averages of groups and there is always overlapping. Both heredity and environment contribute both to differences between individuals and to differences between groups. Having reached this stage, two outstanding questions need to be asked. First, why does Biological Race attract such strong emotions? At a public meeting, if a speaker argues for tolerance and goodwill, someone is almost sure to ask whether he would like his daughter to marry a black man; no one asks whether he would like her to marry a man whose IQ is less than 95. But this would be a more rational cause of anxiety. Why does the question take this form? Secondly—why is this so absorbing a question in Britain but is not liable to be asked in Brazil? The marriage, be it understood, is not very likely to take place in Brazil but the question will not be asked in public. The questions are here expressed in a concrete form, because for my own mind this brings home the point more vividly. But they can of course be put in a more generalized form. Why is Biological Race—rather than intelligence or height—chosen in some societies as a social category on which to base an unequal social structure? Why is it so frequently linked with sexual relations? And why is it that in some societies the social categories, though given racial labels, do not correspond with the biological facts? Why, in other words, in these societies of fluid racial definition, is there such disparity between Notional Race and Biological Race?

To raise these questions is to come to the heart of the subject. In earlier chapters we have reached negative conclusions; the answer has constantly been that race in itself is of less importance than is commonly supposed. But why people *think* it is important is a question to which we can give more positive answers. They are not however simple answers; they are the results of a complex set of pressures, some internal and peculiar to the individual but many external and common to all members of the group to which the individual belongs. This in itself is a simplification; a society will consist of many groups, and not all will feel pressures in the same degree. And the pressures will be of many kinds—social, political, and economic. Some will bear on the whole group; others will be generated within the group and applied to its members. But all these external pressures will come to bear in the end on individuals and each individual's reaction to them will depend on the structure of *his* personality, his home background and upbringing, his conscious values and unconscious desires.

It is the general argument of this book that race relations is a field of study in which no single academic discipline can be allowed to predominate—and the point is here illustrated exactly. Sociologists, political scientists, economists seek to find patterns in the behaviour of human beings acting in groups; psycho-analysts try to understand the behaviour of individuals. But the group is composed of individuals and their reaction to the pressures on the group cannot be understood without some understanding of the pressures within themselves. No individual can exist by himself; we wonder at the endurance of those who survive solitary confinement or single-handed voyages, but they are living on their stored experience of communication with their fellow men; a man who has never been able to communicate at all is an idiot, a word literally meaning a private person, so private that he knows no one else. Each of us is the product of a bundle of forces and influences and in his social life acts a number of roles. But he retains a continuity through change; he is, in the end, a unity—indivisible, as the word individual suggests. It is therefore pointless—indeed, meaningless—to argue whether the external or the internal forces are more important. Is it the volume of water or the force of gravity that makes the power of Niagara? But, for two reasons, it seems better to deal with the internal pressures first; they help to explain the working of the external pressures and it is the latter which can be most easily changed. Statesmen can make laws and have some power to manipulate wages, employment, housing; they have much less opportunity to change the structure of men's personalities. It will therefore be the last parts of this book which will deal with varieties of political, economic, and social situations, with the differences between them, with how they have arisen, and with how they affect attitudes about race.

It is necessary to emphasize a little further the fact that the internal pressures are always in operation when racial hostility is displayed. Consider the case of the young men convicted and sentenced to imprisonment after the incidents at Notting Hill in 1958.* They said they had gone on a 'nigger-hunt'. It was argued at the time by the press in general and by many white people that racial hostility was due to the housing shortage, or to unemployment, or to various similar external pressures. But the youths who were convicted had not themselves been deprived of a house which had gone to a West Indian; they did not allege any specific grievance nor did they allege any offence against the people they attacked. Their victims had not taken a house or a job from anyone; they were attacked because they were black. The cause for this must surely lie deeper than any of the external pressures; housing and employment are merely excuses.

There is an important distinction to be made here. Irrational prejudice of an extreme kind was at work in Notting Hill. But there is a form of behaviour much more widespread in Britain, commonly attributed to landladies, who are reported to justify refusing lodgings to someone not white on the grounds: 'I don't mind myself, it's what the neighbours would think.' Similarly, employers will say: 'It's not that I have any prejudice, but the men would object.' Surely such remarks should not be taken at their face-value; indeed, it seems a plausible hypothesis that when relaxed, in private, with a friend in whom the speaker had

* In 1958, there were outbreaks of violence in Notting Hill, an area in Western London which is socially on the downgrade. Hostility was directed at West Indian immigrants. Many windows were broken and damage done to shops. Several people were injured but no one was killed. (James Wiskenden: *Colour in Britain*, Oxford University Press, 1958.)

confidence, different views would often be expressed. Such a justification, in fact, usually conceals a mild personal prejudice; it is a
response to an internal pressure, masquerading as a response to an
external pressure. But even in the rare cases where this is not so,
the employer's reaction to an external pressure can take the form
of yielding to it or of trying to overcome it and this will depend
on his own personality and the pressures within him.

2 Prejudice and Stereotypes

What then is prejudice? It means literally, judgement in
advance, and, in the context of race relations, seems to be legitimately used of a judgement based on a fixed mental image of
some group or class of people and applied to all individuals of that
class, without being tested against reality. Some writers reserve the
word for the most extreme and irrational form of prejudice, but
this involves a considerable departure from the normal use of the
word and also inventing a new word for mild prejudice.* My
working definition seems preferable and at once leads to a discussion of what is meant by a fixed mental image, or stereotype.

It is perhaps inevitable that we should all, to some extent, form
some kind of stereotype of people who belong to another group.
There may have been some grounds for it in the first place and
the original impression may be strengthened because one remem-
bers what confirms the stereotype but forgets what does not.
Further, in the case of a weak minority, the nature of the stereotype
will be known to the group affected and some members of it will
act out the part in order to win some advantage. There is a story
told by Richard Wright in his autobiography, *Black Boy*, about
a Negro lift man who boasted of his skill in getting a quarter-dollar
from a white man. He would beg for a quarter, obsequiously and
cringingly, and eventually offer to let the white man kick his back-
side while he picked up the coin. He boasted because he had made
the white man feel good by confirming his conviction of Negro
inferiority; by this means he had tricked him and in spite of his
own humiliation could despise his dupe. This was a crude and

* And here they depart still further from normal use, labelling 'mild
prejudice' as 'antipathy'. But this is a reversal of normal values; 'antipathy'
means by derivation 'feeling against' and by common use 'settled aversion'.
(*Concise Oxford Dictionary*.)

extreme case, but in Europe the despised Jew has often played this kind of trick on the arrogant Christian noble; African servants play it on their employers in Southern Africa today.

There is a counterpart to this, considerably more widespread, by which members of a deprived group are virtually forced to act out the part allotted in the stereotype. It is generally known as 'the self-fulfilling prophecy'. A form of it is familiar in schools; a teacher for some perhaps superficial reason starts with a poor opinion of a child and asks a question in a way that shows it. The child quickly perceives that it is not expected to do well and makes no effort. The teacher's opinion is confirmed. This is what may happen in a wider context to an entire group of whom the dominant group hold an unfavourable stereotype. The Negro is poor, badly educated, badly housed. Therefore he is quite unfit for the job that would enable him to escape from these conditions; he is caught in a vicious downward spiral.

But, while some kind of stereotype is necessary if one is to have any mental picture of a foreign group, a sensible person will test his stereotype against reality in any individual case. Two hundred years ago, in the time of Dr. Johnson, the English formed an unfavourable stereotype of the Scots, who, they thought, were niggardly, humourless, clannish and much too hardworking. Scotland was a smaller and poorer country where it was hard to get a living and no doubt some of these qualities could justly be attributed to some of the emigrants who came to London in the eighteenth century. To expect to find all of them in every Scot even then would clearly have been irrational; that would be prejudice.

That particular prejudice, so strong in Dr. Johnson, is not often met today. But there are still men who make remarks about 'women drivers', in spite of the facts that some women win Alpine rallies and obviously drive better than most men, while most insurance companies regard women as a better risk. Such men remember every mistake they have seen a woman make in a car, forget the mistakes they have seen men make, generalize their observations and judge that 'Women are bad drivers'; the final step is to expect to find any particular woman a bad driver just because she is a woman. They do not test their first generalization against reality. Obviously, this kind of judgement constantly takes place about other racial groups.

There may be a number of reasons for this. Mere laziness may
sometimes seem enough to account for it; the picture was stamped
on the mind long ago, no striking contradiction has occurred to
change it, and no trouble has been taken to check. Lack of information and experience will buttress this kind of laziness and it is
liable to be upset by education, particularly at sixth form or
university level, where the pupil ought to be continually ques-
tioning assumptions that have been taken for granted. External
pressures may also be a reason for leaving the stereotype undisturbed; in South Africa, the extreme case, any white person must
be aware that his comfort and wealth depend on a social structure
which keeps all white people above all black and which would
hardly be justifiable unless he could think of black people as
naturally his inferiors. So the pressure on him is strong to let the
stereotype alone. But the third kind of reason, which will also be
present in some degree in the first two, proceeds from the structure
of the individual personality and needs some explanation.

3 Inner Conflict

It is difficult—indeed, to me impossible—to imagine a human
being in whom there is not some degree of conflict. Some may
appear self-satisfied but in fact even the least critical of himself
does to some extent either fall short of his own ideal or fail to
win the approval he believes he deserves. This conflict arises from
life in society; in every form of society there are some acts which
must either be restrained or performed in private. The child is
born as selfish as a plant or an animal; if he is to live with other
men he must learn what he may do and what he must not. This
conflict between self and society—to which I referred briefly in
the first chapter—centres on the parent, or on someone who takes
the place of a parent. The parent is the source of food, admiration,
warmth, love—all that the baby desires. But from the same
fountain—the parent—flow not only every kind of satisfaction,
but also the first frustrating checks on infantile egoism; to the
child this is a shock and seems a betrayal. This is so to some extent
in even the most affluent and permissive of societies; the parent is
bound to prevent the child from fulfilling some desires and will
therefore be taken as a symbol to which other frustrations will be
attributed, even though they have nothing to do with the parent.

The problem for every human being, one which cannot be avoided, is to make a transfer of allegiance from parental authority to personal autonomy. This involves a transition from the code imposed by the parents to a new, personal system of conduct, of rules for life, of ambitions to be pursued. The child may, of course, take as his own a system identical with that of the parents, and this is what is likely to happen in a closely knit and static form of society, such as was once provided by a Hindu village and by many African tribes. But there are nonetheless a transition, even though it may have been almost imperceptible. And, indeed, in such societies the transition was usually symbolized by some kind of ritual. In a modern, individualist and competitive society, particularly at a time when all values are under question, the transition will obviously be much more difficult and the conflict more acute. It will be a far more serious problem to feel confident of one's own identity.

There are various ways in which the conflict in man can be represented. But though few today would accept every detail of Freud's teaching, his account of the structure of the personality and the nature of this inner conflict seem in their broad outline likely to endure. He pictures the Ego at the centre of the personality, conscious of sharing its identity with two other nuclei which at times seem foreign and even hostile to the Ego, the central self, which reasons and struggles with them. One of these nuclei is the Id—the neuter form of the Latin word for 'That', which might be translated into English 'The Thing'. This is that depth of the unconscious into which we banish the urges with which we are born but which we regard as anti-social or immoral. They are not dead; they are there below the surface in the dark pool. There is nothing unhealthy about repression in itself; indeed, it is a necessary condition for social life. Danger will arise only if too much is repressed into the Id and no means provided for the release of energy in forms of activity of which the Ego *does* approve.

Over against the Id stands the Super-Ego, that admonitory being which has taken the place once held by the parent and which reproaches the Ego if it fails to live up to the ideals which the parents instilled and which the Ego—perhaps in a modified form, perhaps reluctantly—has now accepted as its own. But the Super-Ego is regarded by the Ego with the same mixed feelings as were felt for the parents.

As I have said, there are other ways of formulating this inner conflict; for Jung, the archetypal Shadow replaces the Id and bears some resemblance to it. To the present writer, it has long seemed that the Super-Ego, the Ego, and the Id are new ways of describing what in the traditional teaching of the Christian church have been called the Conscience, the Soul, and Original Sin, the latter often conveniently personified as the Devil. This is not an orthodox view, either to Freudians or Christians, but what can, I think, hardly be disputed is that moral conflict, long before Freud, was felt as a struggle within the personality between something felt to be the true self and something else felt to be within the self and yet foreign. 'For I do not do the good I want, but the evil I do not want is what I do. Now if I do what I do not want, it is no longer I that do it, but sin which dwells within me,' wrote St. Paul (Romans 7: 19).

Not everyone wrestles as St. Paul does with an inner force that he repudiates. But everyone feels some dissatisfaction at failure to win approval or to live up to his accepted code, even if, like Claude Brown's, it is the code of a limited section of society, anti-social in the view of the majority. If the Super-Ego does not approve, at least the gang will. And what the Ego constantly seeks is the approval still owed it by those treacherous parents who withdrew their love; for this, a substitute is the victory which comfortingly asserts an identity which the world does not seem to recognize. An easy way to attain that approval and sense of identity is to make oneself utterly one with a gang—and there is no easier way to unite a gang than to display hostility to someone outside it and assert superiority over him.

Crows and hens will attack a sick member of the flock, and this primitive way of asserting the unity of a group sometimes shows itself among small boys, who will bully someone different from the gang. Such behaviour asserts identity with the gang and comforts Ego as to his own identity; it also permits release from the Id of something which had been repressed unwillingly and which can now be let out with a feeling of approval. Aggressiveness must have played a useful part in the early stages of human evolution; when social behaviour came to take the place which natural selection had played at an earlier phase, a distinction appeared between aggressiveness directed outside the social group, which was still a socially valuable quality, and aggressiveness within, which had to be repressed and replaced by loyalty to the common interest. It is possible to regard human progress in the moral sphere as a widening of the circles within which moral obligations are felt; in many primitive societies, obligations are felt only to kin or to the clan or tribe.

The behaviour of those who go out with iron bars to attack individuals of a group they regard as quite different from themselves can thus be explained; it is the release of an aggressiveness that is really tribal in origin. But the people most likely to behave in this way do so for personal reasons; they need reassurance as to their own identity. There is evidence of a higher incidence of prejudice among those who have recently risen or fallen in the social scale. They are perhaps uneasily aware of some personal failure and uncertain of their relations with the society that surrounds them. They see other people in terms of stereotypes, and thus as possessing the clearcut identity which they envy; it is necessary to reassure themselves that the clearcut identity is inferior. The man conscious of a personal failure will tell himself: 'At least I am not a Negro'—or a Jew—or whatever is the object of his antipathy.

The conflict and sense of inadequacy are extreme where the antagonism is crudely violent; where they are expressed more politely or diffidently they are either less strong or more under control. But in either case the mechanism is basically the same. The hated group is associated with the elements in the self which are felt to be hostile, either with the nagging Super-Ego or with the rejected Id. In the United States, the Jew is disliked as hard-working and frugal, too successful and too clever, the Negro as dirty, lazy, and unrestrained, as lacking in foresight. One stereotype represents what the Super-Ego urges the Ego to be—and what he knows very well he is not. The other popular stereotype is of a being who continues to give way to those infantile tendencies which Ego has repressed—and sometimes wishes he could still indulge. Marie Jahoda has pointed out that Hitler succeeded—by extraordinary skill in political sleight-of-hand—in persuading the German people to regard the Jew as at the same time both the Super-Ego and the Id, as too hard-working and successful and at the same time dirty, idle, and sexually promiscuous. More recently, in England, there is some evidence that some of the inhabitants of Southall have changed their reasons for objecting to the presence

c

of Sikh children in schools; at first, it was because they were so backward that they kept white children down to their level, but now it begins to be unfair competition because they work so hard and are so clever at figures. The point was made by R. K. Merton in 1949 that, if Abraham Lincoln worked far into the night: 'This testifies that he was industrious, resolute, perseverant and eager to realize his capacities to the full. Do the out-group Jews or Japanese keep these same hours? This only bears witness to their sweatshop mentality, their ruthless undercutting of American standards, their unfair competitive practices. Is the in-group hero frugal, thrifty and sparing? Then the out-group villain is stingy, miserly and penny-pinching.'[15]

The ancient Jews used annually to lay all their sins on a 'scapegoat' which was then driven away into the wilderness: 'Aaron shall lay both his hands upon the head of the live goat and confess over him all the iniquities of the children of Israel . . . putting them upon the head of the goat, and shall send him away . . . into the wilderness . . .' (Lev. 16: 21). I found a similar practice in a Himalayan village, though it occurred every fourth year and had to be a four-horned sheep which always miraculously appeared in the right year and was driven away towards the high snows; the same kind of custom has also been found among African tribes. It represents so exactly a psychological process which is usually performed unconsciously that 'scapegoat' has become a technical term. A person may project his repressed desires, his failures, his sins on to someone else, whose fault it becomes that things have gone wrong; as in the case of Hitler and the Jews, a whole nation may reject the idea that they themselves bear the responsibility for guilt or failure and project all this on to some minority whom they punish for the offences laid on them. This is one of the most dangerous and sinister phenomena in race relations; as a psychological mechanism, it is present to some extent wherever one group hates or despises another, but its special danger lies in the use Hitler made of it. Is is easy to unify people in hatred; nothing will reconcile the different interests within a nation more thoroughly than a common enemy.

Hatred or dislike for an out-group meets a need so generalized in a modern competitive society that an American investigator found that many people expressed intense dislike for three entirely imaginary nationalities, the Danireans, the Piraneans, and the

Wallonians;[16] some even advocated restrictive measures against them. And the need is so strong that, when someone in real life meets a member of the despised and hated group who does not resemble the stereotype, he will stick to the stereotype as the rule and reject reality, labelling the case of which he has real knowledge an exception. 'One of my best friends is a Jew but then he's not like other Jews,' he will say.

In 1950 T. W. Adorno and others with their book on the *Authoritarian Personality* established a concept which has genuine validity in this field, although probably not the overriding importance then attributed to it. All that has been said in this chapter fits in with the idea that certain personalities feel the need for strong external props, will prefer strict discipline to allowing individual freedom, and are likely to be in favour of the repressive punishment of crime and restrictive measures against out-groups. But today most would agree that the concept of the authoritarian personality provides only a partial explanation of racial hostility. In the first place, the authoritarian personality cannot be attributed to one distinguishable group and to no one else; some elements of authoritarianism are to be found in most people. Secondly, a South African white need not be authoritarian to be a racialist; the social and economic pressures on him are enough. But there can be little doubt that the practice of racial exclusiveness will encourage an admiration for rigid discipline, a rigidity in classification whatever the problem, a severity in punishment.

4 Sex and Aggression

The last points to be made in this chapter are perhaps the most important, though this will be disputed by some. Granted that there is a widespread inner need to display hostility to some other group, why should there be such concern about sex, and why should there be so much feeling about *colour* as a mark of difference? The answers arise from the general view here expressed. One of the elements in the infantile personality which in most societies undergoes some degree of restraint and repression is the sexual. Where it has been severely repressed and no outlet provided, the sexual impulse is often an object of fear and Ego is afraid that it will escape. He imagines an out-group, whom he associates with the Id, as being free from the restraints to which he himself is subject. He has only partially accepted his own autonomy; the restraints came from the parents who betrayed him and the Super-Ego, which he identifies with the parents, is continually nagging because he does not want to observe them. Few indeed are those who accept with their whole heart the code of sexual behaviour which they outwardly adhere to. He looks therefore with an envy which he does not acknowledge, and which he wrongly supposes to be disapproval, at these immoral creatures outside the law. The practices he ascribes to them may be pure mythology, but he wants to punish them for his envy.

This is one part of the sexual aspect, particularly strong in the Protestant peoples of north-western Europe. But it is sometimes part of this same repressive process for the man to put the women of his own class and race on a pedestal. In that case, it sometimes happens that the man is afraid of sexual pleasure with an equal and seeks it in circumstances where he need show no respect; he exploits the women of an inferior social class, who are not bound by the restraints of his own. He has failed to achieve a true sexual partnership in which companionship and common interests are fused with the physical pleasure; his sexual encounters with women of the subordinate group have been almost purely animal and it is intolerable to think of men from that group having sexual contact—of just that nature—with women of his own class, whom he himself idealizes as pure and unattainable, or at least expects to observe rigid rules of conduct. This happens in a sharply differentiated class system as well as in a racially divided society; it is a constant theme, for example, in the writings of Tolstoy[17] as well as in the literature of the Deep South and of South Africa. It lies beneath the surface of Victorian England.

This may produce a number of side-effects. The women of the superior class—envious of their greater freedom and sometimes jealous of the attention paid them by their own men—may be particularly cruel to women of the lower group,[18] or, if they employ male servants, they may take a delight in humiliating the men of that group who are forbidden to them and of whom they are afraid.[19] The men of the upper group may pass laws of a specially punitive or restrictive kind; in Southern Rhodesia, for example, an Act passed in 1903 made it a criminal offence for a black man and a white woman to have sexual intercourse (or for either to make advances to the other). But there was no similar provision in respect of intercourse between white men and black women, which commonly occurred. Attempted rape was an offence punishable by death, and although the law did not provide that this was only applicable between black men and white women, there was never any question of the death sentence being passed in any other case.[20]

There were reactions of two kinds to this from Africans in Rhodesia. There is a good deal of evidence that Africans resented the freedom with their women which the early white settlers took for granted; indeed, several shrewd observers in the first quarter of the century thought this was their chief grievance. But to the jealous protection of white women, the reaction of the unsophisticated tribesmen of this early period of Rhodesian history is said to have been that there must be some very special magic about sleeping with them if they were so jealously guarded. And, psychologically, this is not dissimilar from the very well authenticated reaction of the educated black man, whether South African, Rhodesian, or Afro-American; many will say in conversation—and almost every black writer has said it in writing—that to sleep with a white woman is the one possible revenge against the white man, the supreme assertion of the black man's own manhood.[21]

This leads us back to a general point. For the male, uncertain of his own identity, doubtful of his place in the social structure and of his success as a man, sexual achievement is often the first and most complete means of asserting identity; it is a victory, he is wanted, he is a man. But if this uncertain and essentially immature person has already tried to achieve self-confidence by hostility to another despised group, he is bound to resent a similar victory by a male of that group over a woman of his own.

5 Colour and Prejudice

Sex, then, is close to the heart of racial aggressiveness. But why is aggressiveness so specifically applied to *colour*? Here we enter realms in which there is little certainty and it is most unwise to be dogmatic. There is, first, a broadly Marxian view. Capital needed an outlet, so colonies were acquired; the domestic proletariat were encouraged to look down on the natives of the colonial territories so that they would be contented with their lot instead of rebelling against their masters. Or, to state the argument rather more sympathetically, the inhabitants of distant or outlying territories could be exploited even more ruthlessly than those at home, and with even less opportunity of revolt, while the domestic labour could be encouraged to take part, up to a point, in the exploitation. Association with slavery and with servile or colonial status is thus the main factor in the hostility; colour is merely an accident and a badge, distinguishing people from the capitalist countries of north-western Europe from those with darker skins. Race hostility, in short, is only a by-product of class hostility, and the white proletariat, in order to bolster up the whole hierarchical class system, have been brought to look on coloured people as a class lower than themselves.

There are several elements of truth in this. Colour prejudice is indeed one form of group prejudice and we shall argue, in later parts of this book, that the establishment of a stratified social hierarchy has been one of the means by which rulers have established their hold and been able to set up organized systems of government. It is true, also, that the racial theories of the nineteenth century, which greatly intensified racial feeling, both of whites against blacks and today, in the reverse directon, of blacks against whites, were a response to a *need*, of a political as well as an economic kind, felt by the industrial countries. It was a corporate need, which happened also to meet the individual psychological needs which we have been discussing throughout this chapter.

But the Marxian or class argument is far from being the whole truth. Indeed, in its entirety it seems to me historically untenable, if 'capital' is understood in any normal sense. There were ancient Empires in Rome and Assyria which were hardly capitalist; even modern European colonization began *before* industrialization; the Spanish expansion into America cannot be regarded as a case of capital seeking an outlet but rather the reverse. The Conquistadors did not go to Mexico and Peru to trade or to sell manufactured goods but to find gold and bring it back to Spain as a sign of the glory they had achieved with the sword. Far from colour prejudice being exported from the metropolis to the colonies as a means of imperial control, it has more often been the reverse; in both Spanish and British colonial history, the white colonials have frequently been at odds with the Crown or the central government because it would not permit them to exploit the natives as they wished.

It is then my argument that imperialism and colonialism are older than capitalism and have not necessarily much to do with it. But, what is more important for our present purpose, unfavourable associations with a black skin are older than the industrial system or the form of slavery from Africa which developed in the New World. I have argued elsewhere at more length[22] that *Othello*, which is generally dated 1604, would have been incomprehensible to an audience who had no understanding of colour prejudice. Both Iago and Brabantio are prejudiced, the latter being a splendid example of the ostensibly unprejudiced upper-class liberal who reveals his true feelings when he is told that his daughter is going to marry a black man. Not only that, but the whole plot hinges on Othello's own deep consciousness that there is something odd about Desdemona's accepting him. 'Haply' he cries in a moment of unbearable anguish and suspicion 'for I am black . . .' And Iago pounces on the point, which he has already hinted at. Without it, he could never have played on Othello as he does. There is a further point that in an early and thoroughly immature play, *Titus Andronicus,* Shakespeare uses a black villain who is completely a stereotype, bad in every way, treacherous, lustful, and cruel; Othello, on the other hand, is 'the noblest man of man's making' yet both his nobility and his failings are related to the stereotype of the Negro as generous, childlike, simple. The writer had grown enormously in maturity over fifteen years but did not assume that his audience had.

There is, further Queen Elizabeth's order of 1601 expelling certain Blackamoors' from her kingdom.[23] Her successor, James I and VI, wrote a book in which he examines popular beliefs about witches in his native Scotland; one of the most general stories was that they met in covens presided over by a black man, who was the devil. Yet English colonial history had not yet begun; the colony of Virginia was founded in 1606 and Barbados in 1624; the first English factory in India at Surat was established in 1608; it was not till the last quarter of the century that English trade in slaves became general. Nor was slavery exclusively associated with black colour; white persons were sent to the colonies as 'indentured servants' until well into the eighteenth century, and there were then still lively memories of the enslavement of white persons by Moors in North Africa.

But unfavourable ideas about blackness go back much further than this. The Latin words for black (there are two) both apply not only to colour, but also to conduct; they mean bad and wicked as well as dismal and unlucky; the same is true of Greek, Persian, and Sanskrit.[24] The words for 'white' by contrast mean fortunate, favourable, and, of behaviour, pure, open, candid. This symbolism was taken over by Christianity and religious language has always been full of dark deeds and fair promises, black thoughts and white angels. As early at least as A.D. 200 a demon appeared 'in sight like an Ethiopian . . . altogether black and filthy . . .' The Desert Fathers on a number of occasions were tempted by the devil appearing in the form of 'an offensive Ethiopian' and there is a long tradition of showing torturers—and particularly those who scourged Christ—as black. G. K. Hunter sums up much evidence in the words: 'There was, then, it appears, a powerful, widespread and ancient tradition associating black-faced men with wickedness and this tradition came right up to Shakespeare's own day.'[25] He also draws attention to the converse of this assocation; Bede, for example, asserts that when the deacon Philip baptized the Ethiopian eunuch, as told in the Acts of the Apostles, the Ethiopian changed his skin. It was felt to be improper that he should go on wearing the badge of evil.

Thus we have strong evidence that the association is much older than European colonialism or plantation slavery. That is not to say that it is 'instinctive'; it is due to a confusion between a biological consequence of evolution and a metaphor from light and darkness that has been widely applied to moral conflict. It is an association deep in the culture of Western Europe and in some degree is to be found in many other cultures; Hunter gives examples from Africa wider than those I have traced; it is widespread in India; it is reported from Japan.[26] It was greatly intensified in the nineteenth century by a complex set of factors, among which European expansion and the economic factors were present. It is an association which can disappear when confronted with a reality which contradicts it; this is a point to which we shall return.

Thus, to sum up this chapter, we have certain elements in the structure of the human personality which predispose most men in some degree towards aggressiveness, and particularly towards aggressiveness to an 'out-group'. This is likely to be particularly strong in those who, for any reason, feel more than most people that they have failed in their emotional or social life. It is closely linked with sex; it need not be connected with colour, but in Western Europe there is an ancient association of black faces with wicked behaviour which was intensified in the industrial period by fresh association of blackness with slavery and with savagery.

These were predisposing causes. On these there came to bear a complex set of external pressures which were different in various societies, and which produced very different results. To these we shall turn in the rest of this book.

5
Communities, Nations, Empires

1 Different approaches: history, sociology, anthropology

IT has not been easy, in what we have so far discussed, to keep separate the contributions which fall under the heads of various academic disciplines. We have discussed the meaning of race and have called on biology, psychology, and psycho-analysis, but it has constantly been necessary to refer also to what is essentially history. From this point on, it will be even harder to disentangle history from anthropology, from sociology, from political science, and from economics. We may occasionally hark back to psycho-analysis but in general we shall now be dealing with society rather than the individual, with the external pressures rather than with the internal. In its broadest sense all that follows is sociology, the study of society. It will be as well therefore, at this point, to indicate very briefly the sense in which I understand the differences in approach between history, social anthropolgy, and sociology.*

All three study societies, but history makes a basic assumption about causation; the true understanding of the present state of any society will depend on understanding its previous state. Sociology and anthropology, on the other hand, alike think less of succession in time and more of structure; they regard the structure of a society, its institutions, its internal forces, its myths, legends and ideals, as analysable in terms of *needs*, either those the society now feels, or those it has felt in the past. But this difference becomes more and more one of emphasis; today each to some extent accepts the basic assumption of the other, and each turns more and more to the other's analysis of the society he studies. It is, perhaps, a more

* When I use the word anthropology by itself, I mean social anthropology. To avoid confusion, I usually refer to physical anthropologists as biologists.

fundamental difference that sociology looks for *laws* in the behaviour of societies while history regards every situation as unique and, though it draws parallels, is cautious of applying them with any rigidity. Here anthropology lies between the two, looking certainly for patterns of behaviour, but insisting also on the uniqueness of every society.

The difference between anthropology and sociology is a matter on which there will be much disagreement. It could once have been said that the anthropologist studied primitive societies and the sociologist modern, industrial societies. But this comes to look rather old-fashioned. Today the distinction is one rather of method and style, although there is still some difference in subject-matter. The anthropologist will prefer a group small enough for him to acquire some personal knowledge of many of its members; he will seek as far as possible to take part in their activities as though he were one of their community; he will often have many interviews with the same person, making sure that he understands every shade of meaning in what he has been told and coming back again to points in his notes which on reflexion are obscure, or do not seem to bring out the full flavour of the community's behaviour and what is believed to be the reason for it. But the sociologist will prefer a much larger sample, which will be big enough to iron out individual differences; he seeks a result which can be analysed statistically and will thus provide a basis for scientific prediction. He will administer questionnaires, using a number of interrogators. He will seek to eliminate the subjective, inevitable in the anthropological method of prolonged interview, and may, for example, check his results by administering the same questionnaire a second time to the same sample with different interrogators.

Let us bear these distinctions in mind but plunge boldly into subject-matter which concerns all three, although its first stages we owe to archaeologists and to anthropologists rather than to historians and sociologists. It concerns the earlier forms of human society, their growth, development and contacts, the first meetings of peoples and races.

2 A Sequence in Human Progress

The first point to be made is that one can speak of a typical sequence in human progress—which I will outline in a moment—

but that one must not suppose either that every society will proceed through all the phases of this sequence in turn, or that we yet fully understand why one will linger for thousands of years at one stage while another moves on. But it seems a good working hypothesis that the varying speed of development is likely to be due to external pressures and stimuli and to circumstances of climate and terrain and we shall prefer to look for such circumstances, rather than to assume any differences in inherent genetic ability. In modern times—that is within the last two centuries—Africa has provided examples of most of these earlier stages. We shall look at some of them and then consider the results of meetings between peoples who have reached different points in the sequence. Many of the problems of race relations have arisen from such meetings.

The earliest phase of human development of which we have any detailed knowledge, through contacts with modern men who could write down what they saw, is that of food-gathering groups such as the Bushmen of Southern Africa, the Australian aborigines, some Eskimos, and some of the jungle peoples of South America. Let us take the Bushmen as an example; they live—or lived, for there are few left unaffected by modern conditions—in small groups, usually between twenty and a hundred. They had no fixed villages but moved according to the time of year and the supplies of food; they had no permanent huts, but made rough shelters against sun or wind. They lived by hunting and by gathering herbs and fruit which grew wild. They had the use of fire but not of metal; they had the bow and tipped their arrows with stone or bone.

At the next stage come people who practise agriculture. They need not have the use of metal, nor need they domesticate animals; there was a stage of 'Neolithic farmers' in the Near East and in Europe, and they did not at first keep animals. But in Africa the settled agriculturalists have usually worked iron and kept animals. Then come pastoral people, usually nomadic, who have added one great discovery to that of the food-gatherers and the first agriculturists; they have domesticated animals and have flocks and herds of camels, sheep, goats, or cattle. In Asia, though not in Africa, the nomadic pastoral people are often mounted on horses. They have usually also acquired some knowledge of metals. They have tents or temporary huts, something better than the Bushman's shelter.

At this point, we must note an anomaly; the agriculturalists appear in time before the pastoralists, but they have far greater potentialities. The pastoralists are an evolutionary blind alley; yet they often defeat the agriculturalists in war. But the agriculturalists are really ahead in human progress; it is clear that, from their stage, it is possible to go on to others in which there will be greater possibilities of artistic development and all that we may call, without for the moment defining it, civilization. Nomads do not build great cities and are unlikely to develop writing. But it does very often happen that nomads succeed in establishing not only military but political superiority over agriculturalists and maintaining their rule over them, sometimes for centuries.

An example of this on a striking scale—although in fact both parties were a great deal more advanced than the early nomads and agriculturalists of the last few paragraphs—was the invasion of China by semi-nomadic Tartars, who retained the government until the Empire was overthrown. Or one might include the many invasions of India from the north-west by nomadic peoples from Central Asia. There are more recent examples on a smaller scale among African peoples. One outstanding example is that of the pastoral Tutsi, who are believed to have moved into Ruanda around A.D. 1500 and who, by means of which there is no record, asserted their control over the much more numerous agriculturalist Hutu and maintained it until 1960. The Fulani of Northern Nigeria have a similar story, though it is only a century and a half since they seized power, and their control was less unified, being diversified between a number of Emirs, and had less the air of a racial monopoly of power than that of the Tutsi.

But many other forms of encounter between peoples arose, and again the African continent gives us in recent times examples of a process which, in various but similar forms, must constantly have taken place in Asia Minor and elsewhere, which in America was the prelude to the establishment of the Inca and Aztec empires. Some twelve generations ago,* the Ba-Rotse (or Lozi) people— agriculturalists, keeping cattle, using iron—moved south from what was later to be the Belgian Congo into the country stretching for about 300 miles northward along the Zambezi above the Victoria Falls. This country, like Egypt, is flooded annually when

* Their famous King Lewanika, who died in 1916, was distant only nine generations from the beginning of time, presumably their arrival on the Zambezi.

the river rises; it is extremely fertile and this extra wealth must
have given the Ba-Rotse some advantage over their neighbours;
further, the annual flood involved abandoning the village once a
year and, when the flood subsided, peacefully taking up possession
of agricultural holdings whose boundaries had been obliterated.
This surely encouraged social organization and in fact the Ba-
Rotse did evolve a highly complicated social and political system.
There was a king, who in many respects was a constitutional monarch, leading his people it is true, but interpreting and moulding a
consensus of opinion rather than governing by his unaided whim;
there were three councils, representing various interests in the state,
and a marked variety of links, upward and downward, so that a
man would have interests in the villages of each of his grandparents
and would belong to several organizations, within each of which
he would owe allegiance and a certain loyalty to a superior.

This was a primitive state. Economically, it was very primitive
because there was no means of storing food or accumulating wealth,
though there was a beginning of specialist skills, distributed
between basket-makers, potters, and the like; politically it was
much more advanced. It was much stronger than any of its neighbours. These were loosely organized communities, including in the
group with whom they had social contact sometimes only a few
hundred people and, if they acknowledged ties with other communities, having no effective machinery for joint action. By the
time Europeans came to know the Ba-Rotse they had become a
primitive empire, receiving from their closest neighbours an agreed
tribute, in cattle and young people, and periodically raiding the
rather more distant tribes to the East of them, also for cattle and
young people, but in this case as booty rather than tribute. They
made a distinction between those who came from the tribute
states, who were called 'the honoured', and those whom they
rightly called 'the seized'. But both were eventually incorporated
into the Ba-Rotse people.

Further south was another primitive state, that of the Matabele
or Ama-Ndebele. The Matabele were even more recent arrivals
than the Ba-Rotse, their leader Mzilikazi having broken away from
the Zulus early in the century, and having, after a brief sojourn
in what was later to become the Transvaal, moved on to Matabeleland around 1840. Their kingdom was less politically diversified,
primarily a military organization; indeed, in origin it had been

an army. But it is interesting from our present point of view for two reasons. In the first place, there was a horizontal division, based on descent, between three categories. The highest layer or stratum consisted of the descendants of the Zulus of the original army which had split away from Shaka's rule. Next came the descendants of various auxiliary groups who had joined as allies or auxiliaries on the course of the journey from Natal. Finally, the lowest layer, were the descendants of the inhabitants of the land, whom the conquerors found when they arrived. These three layers kept themselves distinct and not only would not marry from the other groups, but would not eat together. This, therefore, was a stratified military society but also—and this is the second point of importance to the argument—like the Ba-Rotse, the Matebele were beginning to establish themselves as a primitive empire. They too had an established, a persisting, supremacy over their nearest neighbours and sent out sporadic raids for booty to those further away.

It would be tedious to give more examples, but there were, in the nineteenth century, many other examples of such primitive states in contact with less organized people whom they dominated and from whom they took captives. Five hundred years earlier, in Peru, the Incas—previously a quite small and obscure tribe—had, in less than a century, succeeded in establishing their king as the ruler of an empire two thousand miles long, with a complex system of bureaucratic rule, good roads, magnificent aqueducts for irrigation, a system of dividing agricultural produce between state, church, and people and of storing food against famine. It had reached a stage of development that was more like the Egypt of the Pharaohs than like Ba-Rotseland, or even the rather more developed kingdoms of the West Coast of Africa such as Benin and Ashanti. But the African kingdoms were set on this kind of road; if we think of the first stages in human development as food-gatherers, pastoralists, and farmers, the next line of development is from primitive state to primitive empire and thence to classical empires, such as those of Egypt, Assyria, and the Incas.

3 Stratification and Dominance

These later stages mean increasing specialization of function. At the food-gathering level, there was little specialization except by age and sex; every family made its own weapons and treated for itself the skins of the animals that fell to its share. Similarly, though there was leadership, it was a matter of age, experience, and skill, and there was no stratification into separate castes or classes. But, with economic specialization as to making spears, pots and baskets, weaving and tanning, goes social specialization into rulers, priests, officials, soldiers and workers. In the classical empires this has reached an extreme pitch; kings have frequently become divine and the peasants are almost as rigidly defined as worker-bees in a hive. One has only to consider such gigantic buildings as the Pyramids, or the fortress of Sacsahuaman above Cuzco in Peru, to perceive that human muscles cannot have been brought to move these vast blocks of stone without extreme differentiation between those who gave the orders and those who carried them out. Specialization had extended to the craft of ruling, and one of the basic problems of politics arose for those who ruled over groups too big for them to establish personal ascendancy over everyone.

They had to assure rule to themselves and to their children; their riches, power, and prosperity depended on the toil of many peasants, slaves, and labourers, on the courage and fidelity of soldiers, on the loyalty of a variety of intermediaries, officials, nobles, headmen. They had to weld together a great diversity of local communities; the empire had to be one behind its leader in order to meet external danger but—as it must from early days have been obscurely realized—some diversity was of value to rulers who could use one element against another if need be. But the principle of Divide and Rule is secondary to the basic problem of politics; it provides means of dealing with an emergency but it is a recipe for disaster unless there is some degree of willingness on the part of most of the people to obey the rulers for most of the time. Society does not really start with *mutual* fear (as Hobbes argued); it is others outside the community who are feared; even the smallest societies have a community of interest and a feeling of 'we' against 'them'.

In a small tribe, the ruler was usually the personal choice of his subjects, from among those qualified by birth; there is a consensus of opinion in his favour so long as he governs within certain limits of custom and consultation. But where the state has become larger, he and his officials or nobles need an impersonal sanction. Fear will operate to prevent elements breaking away or individuals rebelling; it cannot be the permanent cement. And, surprisingly often, the rulers have hit on the same device. They have applied the sanction of religion to the social system and succeeded in establishing myths which stated or implied that the division of society into separate categories by occupation and descent was divinely ordained. Not all have been so explicit as the Pharaohs and the Incas, but divinity, of a kind, was almost forced on Alexander the Great and the Roman emperors, contrary to the past traditions of their people.

It should be added that all societies so far encountered appear to have some sense of awe—at infinity, at death, at the forces of nature and man's insignificance before them—and have based on this sense of awe some theory of the supernatural and some practical system of propitiating, or at best living with, forces more than human. And it has been an almost universal custom to use this sense of the supernatural as a sanction for a variety of social and hygienic rules which have really little to do with more developed religious ideas. In the same way, this one invaluable sanction was applied to the idea that it was the will of the gods that society should be arranged in layers, and in particular, that the kings and aristocrats were by *nature* different from the serfs and peasants they ruled. This was not easy if they had all, at an earlier stage, supposed that they had a common ancestor. But this difficulty could usually be avoided, as empires grew, by making the whole of the original tribe into aristocrats and debasing the conquered.

4 Early systems of stratified dominance

Discussion in general terms quickly becomes unreal. Let us briefly consider some examples, all pre-industrial, of how this problem of dominance was dealt with. One which—though small and insignificant in itself—illustrates the argument happily is the case of the Tutsi, already referred to as the pastoral people who came to Ruanda some four hundred years ago and established their rule over the agricultural Hutu. Their kingdom was unvisited by Europeans until the beginning of the twentieth century and it has been possible to establish from the memories of living people an account of conditions before any change due to that contact had begun. There is no memory of how the Tutsi subdued the Hutu;

it therefore seems probable that there was little fighting and that the Hutu quickly submitted to a people who were perhaps more united or more skilled in arms. That is surmise; what is certain is that the Tutsi at the turn of the nineteenth to the twentieth century were in a minority of about one in eight of the whole population and that the form of dominance they established was extremely thorough. The monarchy was divine and the cosmic order thought to be immutable. The system presents a sophisticated if cynical answer to what I have called the basic political problem at this stage of development.

There were four separate chains of allegiance and tribute running upwards to converge on the Mwami or King. The country was divided into districts (which again were sub-divided), each district being under the administrative charge of two officials, one for cattle and one for land. Each had a chain of officials below him; each was responsible for collecting and passing on to the Mwami tribute of cattle, meat or milk products in one case, of grain and fruit in the other. Each kept an eye on the other, as did the subordinates in their respective chains of allegiance.

There was also a military organization, covering the whole country, to which every male belonged or was affiliated, with a system of command leading up to commanders of regiments, who were responsible directly to the Mwami. The regiment consisted in part of warriors, of whom all were Tutsi; of herdsmen in charge of cattle, also Tutsi; and of artisans, labourers and porters, all Hutu. It thus formed a mobile self-supporting unit in war, but in peace an addition to the two chains of allegiance for cattle and land. The military organization, like the other two, collected tribute and passed it up, each officer taking a commission, as with the civil administration. The army network cut across the districts of the civil administration and thus provided an additional check on the possibility of either rebellion or undue extortion. A man could complain to his military chief if he was unjustly oppressed by his land chief or cattle chief. And over all these three systems of allegiance, of revenue collection and subordination, there stretched a fourth, not so easy to describe in a word. It has been called feudal, but it was not quite feudal, because in theory it was voluntary and because the goods for which allegiance was given were not land but cattle. In theory, a man could go to anyone whom he regarded as a social superior and offer allegiance, with some such phrase as

'Be my father' or 'Give me milk'. If the superior agreed to accept him as a vassal, he would give him an agreed number of cows, from which the dependent could keep the milk and male calves, returning female calves to his lord or patron. There would also be certain agreed services to be performed, as in the feudal system, but behind the agreed services lay a hinterland of total allegiance on one side and of total protection on the other. The lord was expected to protect his vassal against other lords, or intercede for him with the district officials; he might have to protect him even if he were charged with murder. But the lord might also call on his vassal for special service of any kind in addition to the agreed services. The agreed services were generally reputed to be of more value than the milk and calves obtained by the vassal— but the protection given him by his lord was difficult to value precisely. A man had some choice of lords and his act of allegiance was supposed to be voluntary and could be abandoned. But in practice it would be a bold man who dared to abandon his lord unless he had already transferred his loyalty to one more powerful.

By this system, almost every Tutsi, except the Mwami, was lord to someone and vassal to someone else. A poor Tutsi could always ask protection from a rich, and could receive cattle he could pass on to a Hutu, giving his lord the kind of service suitable for a Tutsi to perform—supervising the work of Hutu or herding cattle, but never a degrading agricultural task. The Tutsis, as an aristocratic upper class, had thus an answer to the problem of the 'poor white' which has been such a threat to white supremacy in South Africa.

Separation between the two groups was not absolutely rigid; a poor Tutsi *might* marry the daughter of a rich Hutu but the Tutsi did not like mention of the possibility—and both Tutsi and Hutu indignantly repudiated the possibility of marriage with one of the Twa, a pygmoid people, only one per cent of the population, who had been there even before the Hutu. The three groups—Tutsi, Hutu, Twa—were physically different, the Tutsis being by repute tall, fair and slender by comparison with the darker and sturdier Hutu. And in fact a difference in average height did exist in modern times, though rather less than it was reputed to be, being approximately four inches between Tutsi and Hutu and the same between Hutu and Twa. But the Tutsi did all that they could to emphasize this and other differences between themselves and the Hutu.

In the first place, they emphasized the difference by training; a Tutsi youth would spend some time at Mwami's court, where he would be trained in the use of weapons, in sports and hunting and in bodily fitness, but also in poetry and legend and in the art of conversation. They were taught the qualities needed for leadership—firmness and justice, generosity and courage. It was a disgrace to show fear or betray emotion; to lose the temper was a vulgar act suitable only for Hutu. Maquet (the anthropologist who has recorded this system most completely[27]) asked both Tutsi and Hutu about the qualities each attributed to the other; he found that the Hutu regarded the Tutsi as 'intelligent, capable of command, refined, courageous and cruel'; the Hutu, according to both groups, were 'hardworking, not very clever, extrovert, quick-tempered, obedient, physically strong'—in fact, very like the stereotype of the peasant all the world over. Asked whether the characteristics could be changed by training and upbringing, both groups answered that only very limited changes could be made; the qualities were inherent.

One other point, trifling in itself, is highly significant for the general argument. The Tutsi professed to eat little if any solid food; when on a journey, they would eat none at all, living on curdled milk, banana beer and mead made from honey—never maize beer, the Hutu drink. When at home, they would eat solid food only once a day, in the evening, all Hutu servants being rigidly excluded; even then, they would not eat the standard food of the Hutu, porridge made from maize or millet, sweet potatoes or yams. In short, they were careful to adhere to a diet as different as possible from the Hutu's, and they tried to make it appear more different than in fact it was. They were superior beings and it was essential that nothing should emphasize common humanity.

The kingdom appears to have been stable for about four hundred years on these lines; the last Mwami was the fortieth of his dynasty. No doubt its stability was due to the ingenious answer the system provided to a number of political problems. The Tutsi were kept distinct from the Hutu and everything was done to encourage the Hutu to think of them as aloof, impassive, aristocrats, above the possibility of human failings such as greed or fear. The Hutu, incidentally, attributed startling sexual powers to the Tutsi males and thought this was because they did no manual work and ate different food. The fourfold chain of allegiance permitted a Hutu to attain some wealth and power, in the lower ranks of the district administration and the system of lords and vassals, but it was almost impossible for them to combine against the Tutsi, or for any of the Tutsi to combine against the Mwami; the overlapping and interlocking nature of the whole system made it impossible to bring together in secrecy any large body of persons with common interests. And the lord's duty to protect his vassals, combined with his need for vassals if he was to be rich and powerful, was some protection against extremes of injustice and exploitation. But, as Maquet rightly points out, the whole system was based on the 'premise of inequality'. It was a fixed and permanent inequality but not gross oppression; Maquet calculated that the goods and services taken by the system from a Hutu farmer were about one-tenth of the produce, which is a comparatively benevolent form of exploitation. The whole system endured because it appeared to be permanent and part of the order of things and the Hutu had little chance of comparing their lot with anyone else's. To some extent, also, this system too was predatory upon more loosely organized neighbours and this no doubt helped to reconcile the Hutu to their serfdom.

On the other side of the world, and on a far larger scale, the Incas followed similar principles in Peru and eventually in territories that were later to become Bolivia and Ecuador, even small parts of Chile and Colombia. Their problem was very different. The whole Andean area had seen a succession of advanced cultures with much communication between different regions, and some similarity in religious cults, in food and habits; the pottery indicates the rise and fall of connected styles over wide areas for close on two thousand years before the Incas came to power. And within this area of rather similar cultural achievement, the Incas quickly found themselves launched on a career far more clearly expansionist and imperialist than that of the Tutsi, who, once established in Ruanda, were content to lord it over the Hutu. But the Incas' policy towards the people they conquered one by one was governed by similar aims; they did not aim to destroy but to *keep* as relatively contented subjects or vassals; they would unite their empire—but keep it diverse; they would emphasize their difference from their subjects.

The Incas deliberately formulated a policy of offering terms of surrender which could be accepted without too great humiliation. At first, the conquered tribes were allowed to retain the worship of their own gods, provided only that they would add a general allegiance to the Sun; they might keep their own chiefs, provided they accepted the overlordship of the Supreme Inca. But some special objects of worship, and the sons of the local chief or some of his near kin—young men who could be trained—would be brought to Cuzco, partly as hostages, and partly to aid the process of indoctrination and integration. This began very quickly and it is astonishing that within less than two hundred years the Incas succeeded in introducing one language, Quechua, in place of an immense variety of local languages and dialects, and throughout the greater part of their vast territory. The only large exception was the Aymara-speaking part of Bolivia. With the language went an increasingly uniform system of administration; people and resources were reckoned up and reports sent in regularly on the state of crops, on the surpluses of food likely to be available. The accounts were kept by a complicated system of knotted strings; the reports were carried by runners in relays, from one staging post to the next, along roads constructed by conscripted labour. Every man was liable to serve on such tasks as building roads and aqueducts as well as in the army. The crops produced by each local community were divided into three shares—not of equal size— one for the Supreme Inca, one for the Sun and its temples, one for the community. Food was stored against famine; whole communities were sometimes moved, either because it was desirable to introduce a reliable, Quechua-speaking group into an area not yet integrated, or because there was a surplus of population in one area and fertile land in another. After a time, the more important local chiefs were replaced by viceroys of the imperial service. In general, what was imposed was a centralized administration, with a swift and intelligible, if harsh, system of justice. But the system operated by means of local headmen responsible for communities who, even before the Incas came, had in most cases probably practised a communal system of land tenure. The individual had virtually no rights against the state; he must even marry when the state said so, making his choice from a group of girls of the right age assembled for the purpose. On the other hand he could perceive that the whole system did operate for the general welfare of the state, of which he was a part. And myth and religion told him it was divinely ordained.

The centre was the Supreme Inca; he was divine and descended from the Sun. The key to the whole administration was the imperial service, of which the cream was the royal clan. In this might be numbered any descendant of the ruling Inca or his predecessors; as the sovereign was lavishly polygamous, the number was sufficient. As boys and young men the members of this clan— all children of the Sun—went through a rigorous training at court, with much the same objects as that of the Tutsi. Great hardships must be endured, long distances run; there were periods of fasting and religious exercises; there was instruction in poetry and mythology as well as the use of weapons, above all in self-control. There was a final ordeal before they were admitted to the service. Thus by training, as well as by divine origin they were sharply differentiated from those they were to govern.

Similarly, the Spartans in Greece were warriors and rulers, trained in ways very similar to the Incas, with courage, loyalty, and self-control as the supreme virtues. They too ruled an empire, though on a small scale; they too were served by a conquered people, whom they had found in the land when they arrived. These were the Helots, farmers, each of whom was allotted to a Spartan whom he was bound to supply with a fixed quantity of barley, olives, wine and vegetables. They were serfs who could not bear arms or leave the land, though in war a number accompanied each Spartan to carry his arms and supplies. There was a third, intermediate, element in the system; Sparta's neighbours, the *perioikoi*, who were believed to be also invaders though of different descent from the true Spartans, were tributary 'allies'. They had surrendered their foreign policy to Sparta and promised help in war, but within limits were allowed to govern themselves. They were in fact what we should now call satellites. But internally Spartan rule was rigid. Every year the Spartan state solemnly declared war on the Helots; the Spartans maintained a secret police, the *Krypteia*, and if a Spartan on this service suspected a Helot of plotting against the state, it was lawful—by virtue of that declaration—to kill him at once. There were many risings of the Helots and the Spartans cannot be regarded as having solved their problem wisely. Theirs was a police state; they set up a statue to Fear in their market-place.

These examples could be endlessly multiplied. They are sufficient to suggest certain generalizations. Human progress is uneven; groups develop at different paces. But it is rare that there should be much progress in internal organization and in economic specialization without a distinction arising between rulers and ruled. This the rulers frequently accentuate, laying stress on the inherent difference between them. A state which has reached this stage of organized stratification has great advantages over its neighbours and will frequently conquer and rule them, sometimes transporting large numbers to its own territory—as the Babylonians did to the Jews—more often establishing some system of collecting tribute, sometimes, like the Romans and the Incas, establishing an administration. Thus social stratification leads to imperialism. Sometimes, as in the case of the Tutsi and the Spartans, a group will move into the territory of another, conquer and rule them. There are very many different ways of dealing with the problems that then arise. But some frequent patterns do emerge. Initially there is almost bound to be a relationship of dominance and subordination, which the rulers may try to prolong and indeed perpetuate, frequently encouraging a mythology of separate, possibly divine, origin. The intensity with which the rulers determine and maintain this division and separation is one of the factors that varies most widely.

These are early forms of relationships between groups who are really divided by the fact that they are at different stages of development. But to the rulers it seems—and they encourage the belief—that the differences are inherent and due to their descent. If there are physical differences, they are exaggerated. This is the beginning of race relations.

6
The European Expansion

1 The Ancient Pattern of Dominance

THE last chapter dealt wth certain forms of contact between groups who were at different stages of social development, but who usually regarded descent rather than development as the criterion which marked them off from each other. It suggests a very widespread pattern of relationship which constantly recurs. But it is not to be supposed that there have not been many other forms of contact, some at very early stages of history. Herodotus tells us that the Phoenicians sailed through the straits of Gibraltar and down the West Coast of Africa and describes how they traded with the inhabitants. They would put a pile of goods on the beach and go back to their ships; the natives of the coast would come to see what was offered, and put by its side the gold they were prepared to exchange. They would then retire to the forest and the Phoenicians would come back; if the offer was acceptable, they would take the gold and go. It is puzzling to see how such a convention would be first established, but the same kind of procedure is well authenticated from other parts of Africa by later observers. But this system of silent trade is so rudimentary a relationship that it need only be mentioned as a curiosity.

There are other curiosities which need not delay us. Sometimes where there is a very low population density, as on the fringes of the Arctic ice, peoples have been found of quite different ethnic origin moving about amicably within the same region and making no attempt to drive each other out or to establish political dominance. Again, a case is recorded from Africa of a pygmoid people living in thick forest as food gatherers in the neighbourhood of a

Bantu-speaking agricultural group, whom they periodically visit, adopting, or pretending to adopt while they are there, the religious ideas and general system of values of the agriculturalists, which are quite different from their own.[28] But it seems doubtful whether these relationships would last if there was more pressure on land.

In Asia, there are many examples of advanced groups, practising agriculture, with an ancient culture going back thousands of years, living in the plains, surrounded by hill tracts in which there are quite primitive tribes with different languages and much less sophisticated cultures. The geographical reverse was often the case in Central America and the Andes, where the hill cultures were advanced and the jungle folk often primitive. Relationships between such communities were usually shifting and uneasy; in Burma, for example, the kings of Burma at Mandalay claimed sovereignty over various hill peoples and sometimes received tribute from the more advanced, such as the Shans; on the other hand, the hill tribes would take advantage of any weakness of the Burmese monarchy and raid the plains. The kings might send a punitive expedition in return but were never strong enough to establish an administration in the hills. A wary hostility was the general rule. In India, there were mountainous areas left out alike by the general Hindu culture and by the Muslim conquerors who established rule over the Hindus; here, primitive tribes held to their ancient ways until far into the nineteenth century. No systematic attempt was made to subdue them, but an early nineteenth-century observer records that the landowners of the plains regarded them as vermin and shot them on sight.[29]

Much has been written about the 'plural societies' of South-East Asia.[30] Here, at a recent stage of history, were to be found societies of different ethnic origin—for instance, Malay, Chinese and Indian; Indian and Burmese; Tamil and Sinhalese—entirely separate from each other in language and religion, between whom marriage was virtually unknown, sharing markets, though usually divided by economic function. At the time when this phrase was first applied to these societies, there were many examples of such communities living peacefully side by side. But this was at the end of the nineteenth and the beginning of the twentieth centuries, when British or Dutch imperial rule seemed to be firmly and indeed permanently established. When it came to an end, the apparent amity ended with it. It should be added that such peaceful existence had sometimes occurred at other periods in Asia, but usually under a strong government and when the minority was in no sense a claimant to power or a threat to the rulers.

More recently a somewhat similar relationship grew up in Kenya, Tanganyika, and Uganda, where Indians—Hindu, Sikh, or Muslim in religion—operated as clerks, traders, and artisans in countries where the vast majority of the inhabitants were African and the rulers British. But again difficulties have arisen with the end of imperial rule and the same is true in such territories as Trinidad, Guyana, Mauritius, and Fiji, to which we shall return.

These are not really exceptions so much as pieces which fit rather awkwardly into the varied jigsaw puzzle constituted by the broad generalization that human progress was for long usually accompanied by increasing stratification, which in its turn usually led to expansion and some form of dominance by the more advanced, more highly organized, and more stratified societies over others that were simpler. Where the expansion was over land masses, or, as in the Mediterranean basin, round a sea that had long been used for navigation, the differences between rulers and ruled in techniques, in style of art, in thought about religion, in physique, were not usually startling, though the rulers usually tried to make them more radical and more permanent than they were. But we now come to an entirely new phase in human development.

2 The Nation State

This new phase bears resemblances to the old. There is still expansion, domination of other peoples and political control. Indeed, it occurs on a much larger scale than before. But there are two great differences. The societies which in modern times expand and dominate are at first still stratified, constructed indeed on the 'premise of inequality', but there is a contradiction at their heart. They have adopted a religion which proclaims the brotherhood of man, and therefore a moral duty, of which they only gradually become aware, to provide some degree of equality; they have begun to translate a little of this ideal into practice in their systems of law. This contradiction at the heart of West European societies becomes even more open when, having established dominance over others, they themselves become nominally democratic. It is from the tension engendered by this inner contradiction that much of their strength in relation to other societies proceeds. But it infects the conquered group who are bound to turn against their conquerors the values they are bound to acquire when the conquest is established.

The nations of Western Europe are a new kind of society—but they soon establish with many less advanced societies the relationship of dominance, with which we are already beginning to be familiar. But the old relationship now takes on a new intensity. In the first place, there is a geographical difference; advances in shipbuilding and navigation have taken the peoples of Western Europe to regions more remote than has been usual for previous conquerors. There is a discontinuity which has not arisen when people conquer their neighbours; the differences between rulers and ruled are more startling than in the past. And this applies not only to social structure, food, clothes, religion, decorative styles, techniques in war and agriculture, to a greater degree than in the other cases we considered; there is also a much more marked difference in physical appearance. Thus physical appearance becomes, more sharply than ever before, the badge of a difference in culture and status.

Let us go back and consider on a slightly larger scale the ideas contrary to the 'premise of inequality' which lie at the heart of these new societies, which produce a contradiction, a flux and a tension within them. In a religious form, the essential new idea is formulated indirectly by the Jews as the fatherhood of God. Their God was at first strictly tribal—'theirs' in the sense that he had created them and they were his favourites—but their religious vision broadened until in the end they saw him, not as one god among many, but as the One God for the whole world, not confined to one country but universal. Christianity made more explicit the concept of the brotherhood of man, which is here implicit. Islam too was explicit on this point; all power is with the one God, who delegates power to men on earth, but before Him all men are equal. The ideals of all three religions were far indeed from their practice; for Christianity, in particular, compromise was a necessary part of the step by which it ceased to be the religion of a persecuted minority and instead became the official religion of the Empire. The brotherhood of man must now wait till another world; the 'premise of inequality' and a considerable degree of stratification ruled on earth.

But the idea was still alive. It was read aloud in the Gospels every day; the Pope ceremonially washed the feet of twelve poor men once a year—and at Canossa the Emperor was forced to prostrate himself before the Pope. From time to time some ardent spirit would proclaim such piercingly subversive ideas about equality and brotherhood, about the blessedness of the poor, that it would become necessary to crucify or burn him. There were peasant revolts, Lollards, Hussites. And even in recognized institutions approved by authority, a form of these ideas made some headway.

The Jewish religious idea had been supplemented by a Greek legal idea—the equality before the law of all who were recognized as belonging to the same category. This was an important limitation; women, slaves, immigrants were excluded from the concept of equality before the law, even in democratic Greek states. It applied only to citizens even in the best periods of Rome and citizens were a privileged class. Nonetheless, it was an ally of the religious concept and in 1215 the English nobles, representing themselves somewhat implausibly as the champions of the nation as a whole, embodied the principle of trial 'by one's peers' in English law.

It would require a separate volume, much larger than this, to trace the conflict between the ideas of equality and brotherhood on the one hand and, on the other, the fact of stratification and the premise of inequality. Jurisprudence was a compromise between the two; step by step, grudgingly, here and there, justice in society came to be seen as some provision of the opportunity for equality. The state grew into the nation; it was no longer a clan nor was its land the property of a clan, nor the personal estate of a king divinely appointed. It became in Western Europe a wholly new kind of society, united, ideally and so far as possible, in language—regional variations being despised and discouraged —in religion, in political allegiance, but, finally, by the sense that it *was* one, that it had succeeded in asserting its identity. It had distinguished its individuality against the great ideal of unity embodied in the mediaeval Papacy and Empire; secondly, it had established unity against its own components, the great feudal fiefholders. Next, it had succeeded either in defending itself against its neighbours or in defeating them. It was racially homogeneous, in the sense that there were no marked physical differences within it, but it was still heavily stratified, socially, economically, and politically.

But from the point of view of the present line of argument, a most important aspect of the nation-state was that it was always in stress or tension. There was first the struggle for unity, accompanied by religious and political wars to settle the nature of the homogeneity on which it would stand; there was tension arising from the conflict between the reality of stratification and the ideals of religion in regard to equality and poverty; there was continual stress between a growing rationalism and institutions which had evolved slowly, as a response to needs no longer felt in the same form, and often embodied in outdated mythology. As a result of this stress, the new states produced men who had an immense advantage when they found themselves in contact with societies which were still based on the clan and the kinship system. They had abandoned the corporate life of tribe, clan and family, and had made great strides towards a more individualist society, towards self-reliance combined with disciplined organization for a common purpose. They had made great strides also—and were later to make even greater—in following up the causal sequences in nature. They sought for causes instead of looking for omens and this made them seem divine.

3 Modern Patterns of Dominance

In any attempt at describing the past the writer is bound to introduce an element of unreality because he must deal with one thing at a time, and this involves separating into their components aspects of reality which are one, and dealing in succession with events that are happening at the same time. In fact history is far more liquid, more continuous, more simultaneous, than any historian can hope to make it seem. Thus there was no static period, the Middle Ages, followed by a highly dynamic period, which is called modern. Movement was present throughout the Middle Ages; there was no single magic moment when Greek thought was rediscovered and a new kind of thinking began.

Nonetheless, one must emphasize the contrast between the Middle Ages, and all that that phrase implies, and the beginning of modern times, with the expansion of the European nation-states. The purpose of this section is simply to emphasize two kinds of multiplicity. The first is the multiplicity of the breaks with tradition; the new events and changes that contributed to the startling effect which Europeans had on the peoples they found in America, Africa and even, to a lesser extent, in Asia. And the second is the multiplicity of the actual expansion itself.

First, let us recall some of the factors that over a period from the middle of the fourteenth to the middle of the sixteenth centuries contributed to the new kinds of society in Western Europe. The Black Death had speeded up the decline of the feudal system—which was essentially static—and the beginning of a far more mobile economy based on contract labour; advances in technology led men to question all kinds of assumptions based on the Bible and Aristotle. Art, which had been mainly anonymous, became attributed to known masters and intensely individual; it ceased to be the handmaid of religion and became increasingly secular. Immense progress was made in astronomy and navigation and attitudes to causation; printing and gunpowder came into use. In 1517 Luther challenged many of the basic beliefs of the Church and a ferment of argument broke out. And the geographical discoveries, which are the substance of what we are about to discuss, themselves contributed to the new spirit. All combined to create a feeling of vivid adventure, of self-confidence, of a determination that anything was possible.

The Portuguese began the expansion. Early in the fifteenth century they were sailing down the west coast of Africa and opening up a trade which brought back gold, ivory, and slaves. By the middle of the century, the capture of Constantinople by the Turks closed the old land route to the East and added a new incentive to Portuguese enterprise. Before the end of the century they had rounded the Cape of Good Hope and established trading posts in the Indian Ocean. They had also touched at Brazil, which, due to the Trade Winds, was a convenient calling point on the way to the Cape. Portugal later claimed sovereignty over Brazil, over great stretches of both the west and east coasts of Africa, over Ceylon, over parts of India, and over a variety of lesser territories further east. But the original purpose was essentially trade; in the earliest days of the sixteenth century, Almeida, their Viceroy of the Indies, wrote home to his government warning them against commitments on shore in the shape of fortresses in India which would have to be defended. He was prophetic; the problem of the

Portuguese Empire was always lack of manpower; its vast extent became increasingly an embarrassment.[31]

Consider the diversity of this one empire alone; in Brazil, the Amerindians were in the earliest human stages, either food-gatherers or in the first stage of agriculture—known as 'slash and burn'—which involves shifting cultivation and long periods of letting the land rest. On the West African coast, the Portuguese were in touch with primitive states and rudimentary empires; farther south and on the east, with some African tribes who were considerably less developed, but also with the Monomatapa, an emperor whose fame had spread far; everywhere in Africa, but particularly in the east, they confronted Arab rivals; in India and China, they met ancient civilizations and great empires.

We shall return to Brazil and subsequent developments in that country; space forbids any attempt at detail for all the parts of the Portuguese empire. But in general the Portuguese gradually developed an imperial theory, which they have been consistent in proclaiming, but in practice have modified or even disregarded. All their overseas possessions, they proclaimed, were an integral part of Portugal, and the inhabitants were eligible for the same privileges and rights as those of Portugal. Their mission was to civilize and to make Christian; in these territories, any person who had been assimilated, who was in fact civilized and Christian, might become a Portuguese citizen and his race was irrelevant. In practice, slaves were excluded and the number of persons who had been assimilated in Africa after four centuries was minute. Those who were not assimilated were subject to special laws, which included forced labour. But the practice was very varied; only the doctrine applied everywhere.

The next great expansion was the Spanish. When Columbus 'discovered America' in 1492, what in fact he discovered was the West Indies; the mainland was still very little known thirty years later when Cortes set out to conquer Mexico. This was an enterprise of a very different kind. The Spanish had found in the islands two tribes of Amerindians, Caribs and Arawaks, both at fairly primitive stages; both were very soon virtually exterminated, by war or by disease or massacre, or by forcing them to work. A beginning was quickly made of importing Negro slaves to do the work for which the Amerindians seemed so unsuited, and the Caribbean islands were then set on the path which, with so many minor variations, they were to follow for the next four hundred years. As in the northern parts of Brazil and the southern United States, the economy and the social scene were based on plantations with white owners and African slave labour. Yet society developed differently in each of these three areas and to the reasons for this we shall look in the next two chapters.

Very different results followed the expedition of Cortes. He set out for Mexico with only a few score companions, hoping to conquer a great empire and convert its people to Christianity, intending to win gold and bring it back. The empire, of which only rumours had reached the Spaniards, was that of the Aztecs; it was politically and administratively less advanced than that of the Incas—more predatory, more military, not at all concerned with the welfare of its subjects—but in some ways technically more advanced, notably in a system of pictographs that was developing into writing and in astronomical calculations. These discoveries were not due to the Aztecs themselves but to the fact that they had established their rule over part of an area where the Mayas before them had made great advances. Nonetheless, the empire of the Aztecs was a classical empire, at the stage of Babylon, or of Egypt in dynastic times; when the Spaniards first set eyes on Tenochtitlan, the Aztec capital, they stood amazed at so vast a city, with its shining temples and pyramids; they were hardly less impressed by the splendour of Moteczuma's court, the gold and silver ornaments and jewels, the brilliant colours of the decorative feather work in which both Mexicans and Peruvians excelled. But they conquered this empire. Ten years later Pizarro overcame the great Inca civilization.

The Spanish were able to defeat vastly more numerous forces for a number of reasons. First, in Mexico they had valuable allies in the Tlascalans, a people who had never submitted to Aztec rule; indeed, by the later stages of the fighting, the Spaniards had almost as many Indians with them as against. Secondly, Moteczuma vacillated in his policy towards them, alternating between hostility and attempts to appease them. This was partly because of un-favourable omens and prophecies, which made him fear that the strangers were divine. Thirdly, he, and all his people, were at first deeply impressed by the Spaniards' armour, cannon, and horses. But too much can easily be made of this; they soon got over their fear and fought hard against the Spanish in the decisive battle of

D

the Causeways and many others. Firearms were still slow and laborious to reload and were of more moral than practical effect against such numbers as faced the Spaniards; their armour they soon discarded, preferring the lighter Indian protection of quilted cotton.

The question of why so few Spanish were successful against so vast an empire, such numerous opponents, is important. And of the reasons just given, the first is slightly misleading. The Tlascalans at first opposed the Spanish; they became their allies only after they had been defeated in battle. As the odds in their favour were then about fifty to one, the question of why *they* were defeated has first to be asked. And the answer seems to lie in mental attitudes much more than in their material possessions. 'In every encounter in which they were defeated,' writes Pitt-Rivers, 'the Indians saw the judgement of Providence and the fulfilment of an ill omen, whereas the Spaniards took their reverses as lessons from which to learn how to avoid defeat in the future.'[32] The Spaniards, in fact, came from the new kind of societies that we have been sketching. In Peru, their task was easier; here, too, omens and prophecies unnerved the Inca leaders, but there was an additional factor even more strongly in the Spaniards' favour. This was a far more centralized state with an efficient administration and, when Pizarro captured Atahualpa—by gross treachery incidentally—he was in the position of a beekeeper who has the Queen in his hive; he was master of the empire.

We shall come back to the development of the relationships between Spanish and Indian in the Spanish Empire. All that is to our purpose for the moment is to emphasize the motives and ideals of the conquest on the one hand and, on the other, two aspects arising from the nature of the Indian societies. If gold and glory were the first magnets for Cortes and his companions—and almost the only interests of Pizarro in Peru—there were ideals as well, openly proclaimed and of considerable influence in the course of the conquest. The Pope had given Brazil and the East Indies to Portugal, the rest of the Continent of America and the Caribbean to Spain; his purpose was to ensure that the inhabitants were won for the Catholic Church. The Indian inhabitants became direct vassals of the Crown of Spain, and remote though Madrid might be, the Crown did endeavour to exercise a responsibility on their behalf; as the sixteenth century advanced, the Crown's responsibility became more clearly defined and the Indians of the mainland escaped the fate of those on the islands.

Again, the Aztecs and the Incas lived in societies much more advanced than those of the Caribs and Arawaks. In both Mexico and Peru it was possible to take over an existing administration, as it was certainly not with unorganized tribes. Spanish rule meant a foreign instead of a native government, but it was still a government and the people obeyed it. There was no need to drive them away or destroy them; they could be made to work for new masters. Secondly, there was much at the court of Moteczuma which impressed Cortes; it was impossible to regard these people as mere barbarians. No need was felt for social aloofness; as I have already mentioned, Malinche, an Indian lady of high rank, who on baptism became Doña Marina, joined Cortes as his secretary, interpreter and mistress at an early stage of the conquest, in which she played an extremely important part. Hardly less useful was Doña Luisa, a Tlascalan princess, who was given by her father to Alvarado, one of Cortes' lieutenants. The children of both these ladies became Spanish nobles; Malinche's son was legitimized, became Marquis of the Valley of Oaxaca and even a member of the Order of St. James. As we shall see, there were many changes in the way Indians were regarded and many regional variations, but it remained true that no attempt was made, as with some of the people we have looked at, to keep the conquerors separate from the people they ruled.

There followed the Dutch, British, and French expansions. Our purpose at this stage is only to emphasize the extreme multiplicity and variety of the European expansion and I shall not attempt to describe them, but only to emphasize two points. The Dutch and British went to the East with similar motives, being maritime peoples who lived by trade; it was trade they sought and sovereignty came in the wake of trade, at first often because unsettled political conditions made sovereignty almost essential for security. Their approach to the problems of empire was very different from that of either the Spanish or the Portuguese. They were less influenced by the Roman tradition and were not at first at all concerned about a mission to civilize or to convert. Nothing could be more different than the attitudes of Hawkins and Roe, the first British in India at the court of Jehangir, and that of Cortes at Tenochtitlan; they are suppliants, ambassadors, seeking commercial privileges.[33]

Even later, when political rule was a fact, it was a point of declared policy with the British not to interfere in religion.

It is also necessary to note that the British North American colonies were of a quite different nature from those in the East; they were true colonies, in the Greek sense, not tropical dependencies, territories where British men and women meant to live permanently. Even so, they were of two distinct kinds, Virginia being an extension of England where younger sons might seek their fortunes and enjoy the same kind of life as their elder brothers at home, the New England colonies being established rather for dissidents from the established church and polity. It seemed unlikely that such different elements should combine, but they did, and the American colonies were lost. This event probably contributed to an aspect of British colonial policy which distinguished it after 1783 from all the others. It was in fact the negation of a policy, a determination to decentralize, to treat each territory on its merits. This has to be borne in mind when one considers the very varied relationships that arose in India, in West, East, and South Africa, in New Zealand and in Australia—let alone, the hundreds of smaller islands and possessions.

One other factor in modern race relations has already been touched on. Except in those temperate colonies where Europeans of humble social origins meant to settle permanently, there was a widespread expectation that in the New World, the colonist, whatever he might have done at home, would not work with his hands but direct the labour of others. But it was only in the areas of the great empires that American Indians would provide labour; in Brazil, in the Caribbean islands, and in the British colonies of North America, they either would not work or sickened and died if they did. It should be added that in Spanish and Portuguese territories, after the first few decades, there were orders of the Crown that the Indians might not be enslaved. Therefore to all these territories Negro slaves were imported. They were usually captured by raids on their homes, made by African neighbours who acted as agents for the European ships which would take them away. This is not the place to describe the horrors of the slave trade, nor the frightful disruption and degradation it caused in Africa. But it is necessary here to mention that it created a new dimension in race relations. We have seen foreign conquerors with native subjects; we have seen imperial powers ruling neighbours;

now we have a whole servile class imported to serve a dominant group who are also foreign to the soil, and whose declared beliefs and ideals are completely inconsistent with the kind of society they have established. And the ebullience, the artistry, the emotional intensity of the captured people also adds something new to human history.

4 The Contradiction at the Heart

Having briefly noted the multiplicity of the situations arising from the European expansion, let us in the rest of this chapter sketch, still in the broadest outline, the developments of the last century and a half and make ourselves aware of some of the questions which need to be answered. This will provide a background for Chapter 7, in which we shall attempt a series of sketches of particular situations.

The European expansion began with the Portuguese in the fifteenth century and continued with the Spanish in the sixteenth. The British were still an island people at the beginning of the seventeenth century, in the course of which their American colonies came into being. It was only in the late eighteenth century that they began to build up an empire in India; it was in the nineteenth century that vast possessions in Africa accrued to them. The problems with which we are faced in the twentieth century—the South African situation, the problem of American Negro–White relations, all the aftermath of European empire—can all be traced back to developments in this period of expansion.

In these developments, it is an essential element that, by the end of the eighteenth century, the American and French revolutions had already loudly proclaimed principles which were utterly at war with the 'premise of inequality' on which the construction of empires was proceeding. There had been a contradiction at the heart of Western society ever since Constantine made Christianity the official religion of the Roman Empire. Now it was openly proclaimed. Yet the United States did not abolish slavery until almost a hundred years after adopting a constitution which proclaimed freedom as a universal right; nearly a hundred years later it was still necessary to organize protest marches in order to win Civil Rights for the descendants of the slaves. The French, indeed, in the first flush of revolutionary enthusiasm, did free the West

Indian slaves in San Domingo, but the mood did not last even till the restoration of the Bourbons. By the last quarter of the century, the French Third Republic was again proclaiming democratic principles at home but annexing large parts of Africa. Britain's domestic record in the nineteenth century included a steadily widening of the franchise, and early in the next century a beginning was made with redistributing wealth by death duties. But if male suffrage was to be the rule at home, why not in India or Algeria?

There was a double consequence to this contradiction at the heart of the Western democracies. On the white side, the continuance of imperial rule faced every white man with a dilemma—of which of course few were conscious. If he believed in democracy for himself, he could justify denying it to colonial subjects only on the grounds that they were permanently inferior, or that they were not yet ready but were learning and would be ready one day. Many took the first course and believed, without formulating the belief very clearly, in permanent inferiority; others—and this was the official doctrine—took the paternalist or assimilationist line that it was a matter of learning, of maturing. There is a distinction between the strictly paternal view and the assimilationist. The British, the most paternal of the colonizers, assumed that one day —a long way off—their subjects would be ready for freedom. The French, the most assimilationist, believed they could imbue them so deeply with French civilization that they would not want to be free. In Britain, a small minority took the third view, that Ireland and India should not be denied what Englishmen regarded as their birth-right. But few were so altruistic as this; the pressure of self-interest was to find some justification for keeping things as they were and was thus towards either the racialist or the paternalist answer.

Those who have read the fourth chapter of this book will understand that in the latter half of the nineteenth century, when the Western democracies were changing rapidly from rural to industrial societies, when many deeply-rooted beliefs were challenged, there were many individuals profoundly uncertain of themselves and their place in society; they will also understand that such people sometimes feel a personal need to identify themselves with one group and display hostility to another. This personal need coincided with the national need which I have just described, the dilemma of the democratic imperialist. It is not therefore surprising that from the middle of the nineteenth century onwards there was a steady stream of racialist thinking and writing, some explicit and some indirect. This soaked quickly down into popular novels and the newspapers; the writings of Kipling and Rider Haggard and a score of others constantly bear witness to the assumptions made by almost every white man of the time, that there was a ladder or hierarchy of racial excellence on which he was at the top.

Nor was this trend confined to the unthinking; there was much in the European achievement in which to glory legitimately. Merely to state the facts, as they stood at the end of the nineteenth and beginning of the twentieth century, was to encourage a pride which could hardly avoid the taint of racialism. Listen for example to H. A. L. Fisher, a former Cabinet Minister and Warden of New College, Oxford, in the Introduction to his *History of Europe*:*

If a comprehensive survey of the globe were to be made, it would be found that in almost every quarter of it there were settlements of European men or traces of the operation of the European mind. The surviving aboriginal peoples in the Western hemisphere are a small, unimportant and dwindling element in the population. The African negroes have been introduced by white men as an economic convenience. Northern and Southern America are largely populated by colonists from Europe. Australasia is British. The political direction of Africa has fallen, with the ambiguous exception of the lower reaches of the Nile, into European hands. In Asia the case is not dissimilar. The political influences of Europe are apparent even where they are not, as in India or Palestine, embodied in direct European control . . .

He goes on in the next paragraph to list examples of the 'incomparable gifts of modern science' which are due to the 'astounding supremacy' of the European—only to point out that this supremacy has not always rested with Europe and may not continue to do so. But this detached reflection would be less likely to occur to most Europeans than the points previously recounted.

If it was hard for the European not to be at best complacent, at worst arrogant, it was no less hard for an African or an Asian, looking at the same scene, to avoid some degree of resentment or humiliation. Merely to contemplate a people so uniformly success-ful was something of a provocation, but to one who was in any

---

* First published in one volume in 1936.

degree sensitive there was worse to come. Consider for a moment the most favourable circumstances, those of a young man brought up by white teachers who are kindly disposed to him and have the highest ideals. They are, we assume, in this specially favourable case, technically good teachers and he is intelligent; he makes good use of what they teach him. But there are two overriding assumptions behind all they do for him. They inevitably assume that they have something infinitely precious—Western civilization—which they can teach him to understand. And it is also implicit that once he has mastered it he will be part of that civilization.

But by the time H. A. L. Fisher wrote his history of Europe, that young man was almost certain to meet a succession of shocks. He might get a First at Oxford and eat his dinners at Gray's Inn, but he would not be received as an equal by white people when he went back to Africa—and only grudgingly in India. And before he went back he would have encountered, in learned writings and popular, in the street and in the shop, more or less subtle indications of the general hierarchy of esteem in which races were placed. And finally, by the thirties, he would already be aware of a deeply wounding assumption and of a betrayal.

The assumption at its purest and most intense was essentially Victorian and Anglo-Saxon, but it still survives in the popular mind and it is not an Anglo-Saxon monopoly. It was a second stage of defence; finding that Indians—to take one example—when given the opportunity, could compete intellectually on level terms with themselves, it became necessary for the English to emphasize their Indians' *moral* inferiority; they must be lacking in character, in stamina, in perseverance, in altruism and the spirit of service. The justification for these beliefs lay in the real difference which had existed between the two societies, and their products, when they first met; the assumption that the difference was inherent in *individuals,* and would persist even after a Western education, had in it an element of the self-fulfilling prophecy. It was likely to affect the confidence of any but the strongest character.

But some of the strongest characters and sharpest intellects did survive the ordeal of cutting themselves off from their native culture, of learning, in a foreign language, foreign habits of thought and ways of behaving, of learning above all the confidence and self-sufficiency necessary to carry them through a constant awareness of white estimates of their character. To the more sensitive of these men came next the shocking discovery that the West had itself lost confidence in its own teaching. This was already apparent in the writings of younger men when Fisher's history was published. By the fifties, the mood was overwhelmingly strong in Western universities, in leaders of thought, in intellectual journals. To the young man from Africa, who had sacrificed ties with his own people and his native habits of thought, it was a bitter betrayal to find that his kindly schoolmasters had themselves been victims of a cultural time-lag and had taught him to believe in values which were already a subject for mockery in the centres from which they had sprung.

What has been said of the young African requires little modification to be true of the young Afro-American. Slavery ended in 1864 and in the northern states the accepted liberal doctrine since then had been that, with increasingly better opportunities for education, the northern Negroes, at least, would increasingly practise Anglo-Saxon virtues, rise in the social scale, come to be more like white people, to whom they would become more and more acceptable. But instead of this happening, the descendants of the slaves found themselves trapped in ghettoes, the income gap between them and the whites increasing. Of the minority who had managed to escape, in the sense of acquiring education and dollars, most met shocks of a similar nature to the young African's. They had acquired the magic that would bring acceptance, only to find that they were not accepted and that the magic was discredited. They turned angrily against all that was white—Christianity, democracy, the rule of law, the concepts of tolerance and justice, even the music and literature of Europe. All was hypocrisy and lies. And what made the discovery so bitter for the intellectuals was the knowledge that they could not exist without what they rejected. There was no going back to what they had been, nothing to take the place of what they had come to admire.

It is in the light of this sense of betrayal that one must understand the passionate hatred of colonialism and of racialism that broke out in the fifties of the twentieth century. It was part of a vigorous rejection of the whole 'premise of inequality', which had once been the almost invariable accompaniment of human progress and a basic assumption of empire builders, both ancient and modern. It is to this that must be related the various movements, political, religious, artistic, which sought at one level, to find a pedigree for the black intellectual that was free from the taint of Europe, at another to find a religion that was not white, or an ancestry in Ethiopia or Palestine. The same emotional and psychological forces have produced the Black Muslims and the Black Jews of Harlem, Black Power and Black Panthers in the United States, the Ras Tafaris in Jamaica, the far more sophisticated apostles of *négritude* in Paris, and all over the world obscure little sects, movements and risings. A sense of being lost between two worlds, equipped with new wants and no means of satisfying them, frustrated and humiliated by aloof and enviable beings who are yet seen to be men, cruel, greedy and lustful as well as powerful —this is the background to Cargo Cults in the Western Pacific as well as to Mau Mau in Kenya. It is with a foreknowledge that this mood will be the outcome that we shall, in the next chapter, dip back into the past and look in more detail at some established systems of race relations.

5 Questions and Hypotheses

Since the purpose of the next chapter is to provide some material for comparison, it will be useful to suggest now some of the questions to be asked and some working hypotheses on which we shall try to throw light. The first of these questions is the most fundamental. Take four societies in which slavery once played an important part, the Deep South,* Jamaica, Brazil, and South Africa. In two of these, there is a rigid rule that a person who is not white is coloured, and that between white and coloured there can be no social intercourse, let alone marriage, which is forbidden by law. In Jamaica or Brazil on the other hand there are many gradations of colour, and while colour is one sign of social status, it is only one among many. Why is this? I shall suggest that there is no single simple answer. Again, in the Spanish-speaking territories, there is immense variation between regions and periods, but in general an Indian is a person who lives in an Indian com-

---

* By the Deep South, I mean a particular society in the United States in the typical forms which it took at the turn of the nineteenth and twentieth centuries. This society, of which Alabama was the most extreme example, comprised the states which had fought for the Confederate side in the Civil War. It will usually be clear from the context when the reference is to a period *before* the end of slavery.

munity and speaks an Indian language. It is possible for an Indian by this definition to abandon his former community, speak Spanish exclusively and in a new dress and a new occupation come to be spoken of, at least before his face, as though he had changed his race. As in Jamaica and Brazil, though in a rather different way, 'race' is here a social rather than a biological category and this needs some elucidation.

There begin to emerge the outlines of a broad generalization about the nature of the people encountered. When European settlers met people at the most primitive stages of development—for example, in Tasmania, in Australia, and in the immediate neighbourhood of the Cape of Good Hope—they treated them as vermin, either exterminating them or driving them to remote mountains or deserts. When, on the other hand, they met a developed civilization, as in Mexico, Peru, and India, they were able to take over the administration, substituting themselves for the previous rulers. But people at intermediate stages—the Maori, the North American prairie Indians, the Bantu—met widely differing fates. How far was this due to qualities in their own society, how far to the situation of the white settlers? Why do white Americans speak with pride of an Indian princess among their ancestry, making so marked a distinction from their attitude to Negro blood? And why do sexual attitudes differ so? In South Africa today, all sexual contact between races is forbidden by law and regarded with sharp disapproval. But it has not always been so. In the Deep South, white men have habitually exploited black women, though exacting the most violent penalties at any suspicion of the reverse relationship. In Burma, and on the West Coast of Africa, white men often lived for years in concubinage with local women with little disapproval by either party, but in other parts of Africa and in Victorian India, this was rare and strongly disapproved. And, finally, we must consider the question of numbers. Is the relative strength of the ruling group to its subjects a determining factor, or even a factor of importance, in the relationships that arise?

These questions relate to colonial situations, in most of which the dominant group is a minority. But there is another set of situations of a very different kind, in which the dominant group is in a majority. Examples are the northern cities of the United States and Great Britain, in both of which white majorities have been confronted by black immigrants. New Zealand is a somewhat similar society, in that the Maoris, though they reached New Zealand before the whites, are in a small minority. In all these three, there is direct competition between the races. The relationships that results are quite different from either those in Brazil or in South Africa and on the whole are still fluid.

7
Some Modern Situations

---

1 South Africa

IN a book of this size it is clearly impracticable to give any detailed account of the complicated relationships that have arisen between racial groups in many different countries. The relationships always are complicated; they are never as simple as they seem. No summary can be a substitute for more detailed study. Yet to try to compare varied situations without some account of them means assuming a knowledge that not every reader will possess. It seems therefore worth attempting some brief sketches, of particular situations, which will emphasize the points relevant to the general argument, and particularly to the questions and hypotheses asked in the last chapter. In each section we shall try to describe the essence of the present situation and consider how it came about.

South Africa today, as is well known, is the most extreme example in the world of a white minority in power, and determined to stay in power, rigidly keeping themselves distinct from the non-white majority. This they do, first, by laws which forbid marriage between the races and also any kind of sexual contact outside marriage. The law further forbids association between the races in many other ways; education is separate, even at the university level, and travel in public conveyances; trade unions are segregated and a wide range of posts are reserved for white people only. No African may vote or sit in Parliament. Africans have no right to combine in a strike and the level of African wages for manual workers varies around one-seventh of that for white manual labourers. Whites are outnumbered in a ratio of about 1 to 5; about 13 per cent of the total land area is reserved for African occupation and only in these areas may Africans own land or houses; whites may not. In the neighbourhood of towns, where labour is required, certain areas are set aside for Africans to occupy but they usually live in houses rented from the municipality or from their employers, which they must leave if they lose their job. An African is liable to arrest and punishment if he is without documents to show that he has a valid reason for being outside the African reserves. It is a valid reason that he has employment; he can also for short periods have a permit to seek employment. If no valid reason can be proved, he may be ordered to return to a place of origin which in some cases he may not have visited for many years. This is enforced even if it divides man and wife. In short, the purpose of legislation is avowedly to keep the races apart, at whatever expense to personal dignity or family life, and to ensure that no white person ever has to obey an African.

I do not propose to deal with the measures that are employed to keep this situation in being. It need only be said that clearly such a system could only be maintained either if the subject population could be persuaded, as in the ancient empires, that it was immutable—which today would mean being kept in complete ignorance of the rest of the world—or by the rigorous use of force and searching police methods. The latter course has inevitably been chosen and it is the law—and the practice—that a person suspected of a political offence, or of planning an offence, or of knowledge that might lead to some offender, may be kept in prison for long periods without trial. It is a political offence to spread communism, a term so widely defined that it includes advocating universal adult suffrage. There is no statue to Fear in the market-place but, as with the Spartans, fear drives men to harsh and brutal acts.

Nor will it be possible to consider the complications introduced into the scene by the presence of the Indian population and the Coloured, which in South Africa means people of mixed race. The Coloured are allowed some concessions which make them marginally better off than the African, to whom they are therefore suspect. Indians also are inevitably suspect to Africans and in some ways are worse hit than anyone by recent legislation enforcing separate areas for housing. But in essence the conflict lies between about two million whites and about eight million Africans. The question to be answered is how it happened that this line of division came to be chosen and insisted on so rigidly. It can only be understood in the light of history.

The first Dutch at the Cape were officials of the Dutch East India Company, posted there to provide a place of refreshment for ships on their way to the East. The inhabitants of the Cape Peninsula were primitive people, Hottentots, closely akin to the Bushmen and only slightly more advanced. They would not sell their cattle nor come to work for the Dutch, who therefore brought out peasants from the Netherlands to farm and sell provisions to the ships. Relations were poor from the start; the Dutch seldom had a good word for the Hottentots, whom they usually referred to with some such epithet as 'brutal' or 'stinking'. The Hottentots stole Dutch cattle; on the other hand they considered that the Dutch were stealing their land. Over the next two centuries their tribes were pushed eastward and gradually broken up until they had virtually ceased to exist, the surviving Hottentots being by this time domestic servants or farm labourers, and in many cases merged in the Coloured or mixed population.

Meanwhile, the Dutch imported slaves from the East Indies and from other parts of Africa. They expanded from the Cape Eastward and northward, carving out great farms of several thousand acres, a sturdy, simple, self-reliant folk, a frontier society, encountering with increasing frequency people very different from the Hottentot and the Bushmen, Bantu-speaking tribes, who kept cattle, practised agriculture, and worked iron. They, like the Dutch, needed plenty of room for their herds and for their agriculture; they too were expanding but in the opposite direction, westward and southward. There were many frontier wars— 'Kaffir Wars' the Dutch called them, borrowing, ironically enough, from the Arabs a word which the Arabs would apply to Christians. But there were scores of lesser incidents, raids, cattle-thefts, reprisals, frontier incidents. No Afrikaner in the nineteenth century could have failed to hear stories of murders, massacres, the gallant defence of a farm, bloody reprisals.

But Cape Town was far from the expanding frontier and here, after the first few years, perils of actual attack were remote. It was natural, indeed inevitable, that a sharp social line should have been drawn between Dutch and Hottentot; they were manifestly different. But though only one case is recorded of marriage with a baptized Hottentot woman, sexual contact must have taken place, as the Cape Coloured bear witness; in 1657 there were 134 Europeans at the Cape of whom only six were women. In 1671 it is recorded that only a quarter of the children born to slave women were supposed to be fathered by slaves. The question began to arise of how children of mixed race were to be regarded. And again what was the position if a slave was converted to Christianity and baptized? Must he be released? At first, it was felt that he should, but this opened the way to obvious abuse and considerable financial loss. It was hardly justifiable to withhold baptism; it was therefore decided that a Christian *could* be kept a slave. It had seemed as though the dividing line might be between Christian and unbeliever—but with this decision, the chance disappeared. Then slave and free seemed to provide two clear cut categories; MacCrone records the case of a 'free black' sitting down at table with whites in a Dutch farm-house in the seventeenth century.[34] But to this there was the fatal objection that Malayan slaves, and indeed African slaves from the west coast, were far more 'civilized' —that is, amenable to European ways—than the surrounding Hottentots, few of whom were actually enslaved. Further, the original Netherlanders soon came to be reinforced by French Huguenots, with whom they clearly had far more in common than with either slaves or Hottentots. The overriding social distinction thus came to be between white and non-white.

In this decision, I suggest that both sex and religion played an important part. Both Netherlanders and Huguenots were Calvinists, accustomed in their theology to a rigid categorization between the elect, predestined by divine grace for salvation, and the damned; it was not hard for them to make a superficial, perhaps unconscious, analogy, equating white and saved, black and damned. And they were imbued with the teaching of St Paul, who gives a somewhat grudging approval to marriage, but relentlessly denounces sex outside marriage. The encounters between those first predominantly male settlers at the Cape and Hottentots or slave women can have included no element of companionship or shared interests; short, brutal and animal, they would be remembered with shame by people with a strong sense of duty and religion. This accounts, I believe, not only for the classification of their own children as Coloured and beyond the pale, but also for the horror and fear which the Afrikaner nation in general feels at the thought of such contacts today. It will be seen that there is here a self-intensifying spiral; an act which has produced shame because there was no love or companionship in it is forbidden—and it therefore becomes possible only in circumstances which almost certainly ensure that it will continue to be furtive, hurried, and loveless.

The Cape came under British sovereignty during the Napoleonic wars. Three new elements were introduced, British officials, missionaries, and settlers. The official view was that, while the native peoples of South Africa were manifestly backward, there was no reason to suppose they would not improve with education. British officials are likely to have been unconsciously influenced by the British class system; they considered that it would be unwise to make rigid distinctions. The law was officially colour-blind, but the normal working of the social system would reduce embarrassment to a level that was tolerable. No doubt it would sometimes be necessary to ask to Government House people whom one would hardly expect to receive at home, but that was inevitable and movement would be towards a graduated society—with officials from Britain at the top of the scale. British missionaries, on the other hand, sometimes took a far more radical line and emphatically proclaimed the brotherhood of man. The third British element, those who came to settle, in business or as farmers or artisans, tended, like the officials, to feel that time would blur differences, but for the present were seldom any more ready than the Afrikaners to contemplate any social contact. If they were less often cruel, they were more often aloof, which was perhaps resented the more. But they were much more inclined to be lazy in politics; after all, they could go back to Britain.

The British have been inclined to look on the history of South Africa in terms of opposed ideals, either of imperial progress and development against obscurantist separatism, or of British ideals of justice, democracy and freedom against the rigid racialism of the Afrikaners. Both contrasts express some elements of truth but it is more realistic to think of the essential struggle as lying between the Cape and the Frontier. At the Cape, British paternalism was the official attitude until 1910 and the law was colour-blind. It was easy-going, complacent, no doubt over-optimistic; but the franchise did permit Africans and Coloureds to vote in small numbers, and it was left to custom and convention to dictate the degree of segregation. In the Transvaal, on the other hand, an

article of the constitution proclaimed that the people would permit no 'equalizing' between white and coloured in Church or
State. At the Cape, many Afrikaans-speakers supported the less
rigid view and indeed fought on the British side in the South
African War.

When military victory came to be translated into terms of peace,
there was in Britain an overwhelming desire to cement a new
allegiance by generosity to the Afrikaners and, in the course of
negotiations, it was the Africans who suffered; they were a third
party who were not represented. The British Government assumed
that their own paternalist view—so essentially reasonable—would
prevail and the frontier spirit of the Transvaal would disappear.
In fact, of course, it was the Frontier spirit which won. Africans
have lost all political rights, the Coloured almost all. Since 1949
legislation has been increasingly repressive and the enforcement
of the law even more severe. The victory of the Frontier view
occurred largely because those who held it believed in it passionately. No one could believe with passion in the form which the
traditional British view came to take when expressed in politics
by the United Party. It was a policy based less on principle than
on the negative concept that it was a mistake to draw attention
by rigid rules to a separation between the races that was inevitable
for many years to come.

To the typical Transvaaler, this has seemed spineless and
immoral. He felt himself completely cut off from the Low
Countries. The Afrikaners were a new nation, a peculiar people,
with 'nowhere else to go', threatened not only by a sea of black
barbarism but by the uncomprehending liberalism of the British,
which could only end in disaster, the submersion of the Afrikaner
concept of life. Separation must be elevated into a principle and
made a reality. A few went further and recognized that on moral
grounds the permanent subjection of the Bantu-speaking peoples
was wrong. For them, as well as for some who made more cynical
calculations, and for many who did not think very deeply, the
Doctrine of Separate Development had a strong appeal. The two
races could not *share* power; their cultures were still too far diverse.
One or the other must have power—and if it is *they* who have the
power there is no reason to suppose, wrote the South African
Bureau of Racial Affairs as long ago as 1952, that 'the Bantu will
act differently and more fairly towards the European population

than the Europeans were or are prepared to be towards the Native population.'[35] It follows that they must have homelands of their own, where they may develop on their own lines; they will be second-class citizens in the white areas, as the whites will be in the Bantu homelands.

The most obvious weakness of this plan as a salve for sore consciences is that the land is divided in the proportion of about one-sixth of the area for four-fifths of the population. But, even on its own assumptions, there are many other objections. A commission appointed to make practical recommendations for implementing the scheme found that it would require a heavy injection of capital into the 'Bantu homelands' if they were to have any semblance of self-sufficiency; this has not been forthcoming. The homelands are divided and badly placed for communications and markets; the industry and minerals are in the white area.[36] Blacks in large numbers must go to the white areas; very few whites need ever go to the black areas. This scheme, even if fully implemented, would never end white dependence on black labour; no impartial observer who has studied the question can believe that Separate Development would really end the grievance of millions of black workers in the white areas who are denied the right to vote, to speak, to combine, to move freely, to own property.

We have seen how a sharp line was established between white and black and how rigid are the precautions that have been taken to prevent it blurring. There was another possibility that the line should, in Michael Banton's phrase, tilt. If this occurred, there might still be no social mixing, but a man of high status in the subordinate group might in some circumstances be favourably placed in comparison with a man of lower status in the dominant group. In Banton's example, a black doctor in the United States may have his car filled at the petrol pump by a white attendant. South Africa has endeavoured to prevent this tilting of the line by adopting a 'civilized labour policy'. This is known in action as 'job reservation'; many posts are reserved for white workers and may only be filled by Africans on sufferance if whites are not available. It is an example of the corrupting influence of this social structure that the white trade unions have been among its strongest supporters and, indeed, by insisting on 'no dilution of labour', have been largely instrumental in setting it up.

2 The Deep South

Of the British colonies of America, those in the south quickly settled to a slave economy. The American Indians were not subjects of a classical Empire, as in Mexico and Peru, but were semi-nomadic tribes, hunting and practising agriculture. As communities, they were driven westward; they could not, as communities, be enslaved or subjected or forced to work. Individuals might occasionally leave the tribe and, as hunters or in some menial capacity, become a marginal element in white society. This was possible because it happened only rarely and because by leaving the community the Indian ceased to be a threat.

At first, there were white indentured servants as well as black slaves. Here, too, it might have been thought possible that a graduated society would emerge, with a variety of levels. But a number of factors operated against such an outcome. In the first place, as already suggested in Chapter 4, the English were already to some extent prejudiced against black skin; that from early times in America this feeling was present is shown by the fact that in 1630 in Virginia a white man was ordered to be soundly whipped in public because he had 'defiled his body' by intercourse with a Negro.[37] In the second place, even in Virginia and long before the independence of the colonies, there was a much stronger strain than in England of the egalitarian views that were later expressed in the American Constitution; by the eighteenth century, the doctrines of the Enlightenment and the Age of Reason were fashionable. The 'premise of inequality', accepted everywhere in Europe as constituting some kind of deep innate difference between 'gentle' and 'simple', was here much weaker. And, paradoxically, this operated to the disadvantage of the slave. In a graduated, stratified society, it is safe to release a slave; he will still be at the bottom of the ladder. But if there is a feeling abroad that all free men, though perhaps not equal, have many rights in common, then the black man had better be kept a slave. By the middle of the nineteenth century, there were Americans who argued that if all men were brothers, the Negro could not be a man.

This point needs some qualification. It is not to suggest that the Southern gentleman, the large estate owner, did not feel himself distinct from the 'poor white trash', the 'crackers'. But there was a certain bond between them; the poor white sharecropper in

Faulkner's novels can sit and talk to the Colonel in a relationship that would not have been possible between their English counterparts at the same period. Further, long before the end of slavery, power was expressed through politics and voting; the Southern gentleman, if he was to keep power, must win votes and the easiest way to do this was to confine the vote to the poor whites and flatter them by distinguishing them sharply from the blacks. Negro slavery, said Jefferson Davis just before the Civil War, 'raises white men to the same general level . . . dignifies and exalts every white man by the presence of a lower race'.[38] After emancipation, there was a brief hesitation as to the possibility of making a political alliance with the former slaves against white populists —but it quickly disappeared. The populists abandoned their radicalism and made common cause with the gentry; the whites were united.

Again, in the development of their slave code, the colonists were left almost wholly uncontrolled. English law took no cognizance of slavery; in 1772 Lord Mansfield held that it was wholly repugnant to English institutions. The colonists therefore could make their own law, and it treated the slaves as chattels. Their owner had absolute discretion over them in respect of food, hours of work, punishment, housing, sale. The law discouraged either the education or the freeing of slaves; in Virginia, a freed slave must leave the colony within twelve months or be sold for the public benefit; one reason for this, of course, was that the existence of free blacks must make it easier for an escaping slave to be concealed, but it was surely a deeper reason that the existence of free Negroes would blur the one line on which it was safe to stand. The children or grandchildren of a slave woman were all the property of the master; so was any property a slave might acquire. Thus a slave could not buy his freedom, as under Roman law and in the Spanish and Portuguese colonies. During the nineteenth century, the rise in the price of slaves helped to strengthen the system; for some estates, breeding and selling slaves was an important part of the business. Marriage, or indeed any permanent union between slaves, was discouraged; it was thought that fertility was greater if the women were promiscuous and sales were obviously more convenient if any such attachments were ignored. In all this, Parliament in England played no part; nor did the Church exert any noticeable influence. The Anglican Church had no firm central control and in Virginia, instead of the parson holding a freehold of his living, he depended on the continued support of his parishioners at the annual vestry meeting.[39]

So rigid was the legal system before the Civil War that personal contact was not feared. The line between white and non-white coincided with the line between free and slave. It was sometimes possible, with complete safety, to establish affectionate, if unequal, relations with an old nurse or other house slave—and much Southern mythology clustered round such cases, ignoring the far greater number of field hands who, to all intents and purposes, were farm equipment. But with emancipation, it became necessary for the whites to be far more careful; since the difference was no longer legal, it must be underlined more heavily. Common human nature must not be admitted; it is after freedom that segregation in public transport and public places begins. Politically, the South, until quite recently, decided to have one party for which all white men would vote, the real election taking place in the party primary where the candidate was chosen. In flagrant defiance of the Federal Constitution, the Negro was excluded from the franchise, by a variety of tricks or, in the last resort, by a white man with a shotgun under his arm. Thus, as has often been said, though with only partial truth, the Southern white disfranchised himself in order to disfranchise the black.

An elaborate system of manners grew up, designed to emphasize the separation and subordination of the Negro. In this traditional system, the Negro must remove his hat and say, 'Sir', when speaking to a white man, he must go to the back door of a house occupied by whites, however humble, he must not attempt to shake hands or show the least sign of equality or familiarity. The white man will address him by his Christian name, never say 'Mr.', wear his hat if he enters a Negro home. With this went a tradition of sexual freedom for white men with black women, going back to slavery but continuing. It is a tradition of casual exploitation, not of faithful concubinage nor of marriage. The reverse to it is extreme violence at the least suspicion of sexual familiarity towards a white woman. 'Lynching' meant that the crowd would not wait for trial but would drag the accused from gaol to kill him, sometimes with extreme cruelty, by burning alive. This has not happened in South Africa or Southern Rhodesia, though there have been several cases where it has nearly happened. On the other hand, in all three areas, white opinion often seems to suggest that if a white woman says that a black man has looked at her with sexual intent, a black man ought to pay for it, without too much concern about whether he was actually guilty.[40]

There is a vast literature on the Deep South. This is only a brief note of the main points in the system which affect the argument of this book. It is necessary only to add that in the states which fought on the Confederate side in the Civil War, the proportion of white to black is about four to one; on the other hand, in some counties of Alabama and Mississippi and in Washington, DC, the blacks are in a majority. In the formation of Southern attitudes, it must be supposed that hostile pressure from the North has had a hardening effect, just as in South Africa pressure from Britain has added to the deep fundamental insecurity of the whites.

3 Spanish-speaking America

This section will deal with that part of Spanish-speaking America where there were formerly high cultures, Aztec, Maya, and Inca. From what has been said already, it will immediately appear that we are looking at something quite different from the meetings of Dutch and Hottentots, of English colonists and Redskin tribes; here a small body of Conquistadors attacked and conquered great empires. Nothing could be more complete than the conquest; the temples were dismantled, the books (in Mexico) were burnt; native institutions were destroyed except in so far as they were useful to Spanish purposes. It would be hard to exaggerate the shattering and brutalizing effect of the conquest, particularly in Peru, where the native government, though far indeed from mild, was firm, efficient, and basically benevolent. The Indians had lost all they believed in; their view of time contributed to this despair, because in both empires there was a deep-rooted belief that time had to be continually renewed; there were a series of ages in which different forces held sway. Periodically all fire in Mexico must be extinguished and re-lighted with fire kindled by the monarch. Now all the fires were out; an age had ended.

Let us put for a moment the case against the Conquest, concentrating on the Indians who remained in Indian communities. The number who were able to keep their communal lands everywhere diminished during the next four centuries through

European encroachment; more and more of these self-contained communities were changed into villages of 'peons' living on land which had been sold or granted by the State to a Spanish-speaking person. The landowners exacted labour from their tenants in lieu of rent; the amount of labour enforced differed from region to region; in Peru it was usually 180 days in the year but in parts of Ecuador the *huasipungero,* as he was locally called, was supposed to work for his landowner until four o'clock every working day. Landowners commonly made advances of money which the peon or tenant could never repay; interest mounted until he was crippled with debt, tied to the land, virtually a serf. The poverty and degradation in some of these estate villages became extreme during the nineteenth century; it was not always any better in the communities which had kept their communal lands. From any of these communities, escape into a wider world was difficult; it was not of course always desired, but if it was, the Indian who made his way to the town would be treated with contempt as ignorant or stupid; indeed, throughout these countries the word 'indio' normally carries strong derogatory implications. It means doltish, clumsy, rustic.

Let us look now at the other side of the picture. The Spaniards came from a hierarchical, stratified society, in which the 'premise of inequality' was strong. Distinction between persons was hereditary, but it was not expressed in biological terms, and this for reasons special to the history of Spain. The year when Columbus reached America was also the year when the last Moorish kingdom, that of Granada, was conquered by the Catholic Kings, Ferdinand and Isabella, who by their marriage had united Aragon and Castile. Moorish rule was ended in Spain—but the country had been through five hundred years of war; it had only lately been a mass of small kingdoms, Christian and Moorish. There were still Jews, Christians, Muslims. The problem of all others was to unite it— but on what basis? Crown, Church, Nobles, People—these were the pieces on the board.

In what appears a great historical decision, the Crown decided to unite on the basis of Catholicism, not abrogating the *fueros* or local privileges but, where possible, enlisting both Church and People as allies against the Nobles. It was a policy to which the Crown adhered with consistency for a century and a half. The Jews were expelled from Spain in 1492, the year Granada was defeated; the undertakings permitting Muslims to remain in the Kingdom of Aragon were withdrawn in 1524 and a decree of forced conversion was promulgated; pressure increased on those suspected of returning secretly to either the Jewish or the Muslim faith which they had abjured. It was a matter of pride to be an 'old Christian', that is, one whose ancestors had never accepted Islam—a point on which Sancho Panza insists in a tone characteristic of the 'poor white'. It was an essential qualification for some offices to prove *limpieza de sangre*, purity of blood, which meant no Muslim or Jew in one's ancestry during the four previous generations. Finally, but this was not till the seventeenth century, the Moriscos, that is, former Muslims converted to Christianity, were expelled.

The importance of this for the Americans was twofold. In the first place, stress was placed on *belief*, not on biology. There was a confusion, strange to moderns, in the concept of purity of blood depending on the beliefs of one's ancestors, but this background to the minds of the Conquistadors opened the way to a more flexible approach to the offspring of Spanish and Indian. The Conquistadors had lived in a country where Muslims were still tolerated; when their first children were born, from Indian mothers who had been baptized, they had good precedent in Spain for treating them in the same way as the Moriscos, the converted Moors. Secondly, the Pope, as has already been pointed out, had authorized the American conquests of the Crown of Spain and the Church was 'deeply imbued with the idea that the basis of the right of the Spaniards to be in America was their capacity to bring the Indian within the fold of the Faith'.[41]

A contrary view was sometimes put forward and in the middle of the sixteenth century a public and official debate was staged between Sepulveda, who held that the Indians were in Aristotle's phrase 'slaves by nature' and Las Casas, who maintained the orthodox view of the Church, that they had souls, ought to be saved and should not be enslaved. The views of Las Casas were officially supported and the orders of the Crown against enslaving Indians became more strict. A code summing up the laws protecting the Indians was promulgated by Philip II later in the century. Add to this the Crown's suspicion of great hereditary landowners and the fact that Indians were made direct vassals of the Crown; here is the basis for the protective attitude to the Indians which Crown and Church adopted in Mexico and Peru, though they were too late to save the islanders and, even on the mainland, were far from being able to give it effect as they wished.

Thus, the regulations for the first *encomiendas* or grants of land were careful to ensure that they should not be the absolute property of their holders. They were trusts; the trustees were to convert, instruct, and civilize their Indians, who in return were to give them some days' work. The trust was for a limited period and the holder must not live on the trust territory, where he might tyrannize over the inhabitants or lead them against the Crown. The best side of the intention is expressed in the phrase *republica de los Indios*, the commonwealth of the Indians; Spanish Viceroys were entrusted by the Crown with the well-being of this Commonwealth, which was conceived as one of two Commonwealths, for Indians and Spanish, existing side by side under the paternal care of the Crown. But the forces of greed on the spot were stronger than those of benevolence at a distance; the *encomiendas* were gradually replaced by *haciendas*, which were not trusts but estates, heritable not for one or two generations but for ever. Early in the nineteenth century, the colonies achieved independence from Spain, which put political power into the hands of the *hacendados*, and for the Indian ended the protection of the Crown. As the century progressed, fashionable economic doctrine, in the name of progress and the laws of the market, approved of the conversion of Indian communal lands into individual holdings. In the greater part of Mexico, Indian communal lands virtually disappeared, until the Revolution of 1911, when the tide turned and a beginning was made with the creation of *ejidos*. In the *ejido*, the arable land was usually divided into holdings, theoretically of equal size, which an individual cultivated on behalf of the community, while there were common rights in the grazing and forest. It was a return to the principle of the Indian villages of the seventeenth century—but meanwhile the villagers had lost their language and their Indian identity.

We must return to the children of the Conquistadors. Much of course would depend on circumstance; when a town fell by assault, no doubt children would be sired on Indian women whom the Spanish fathers never saw again, and such children would grow up as Indians. At the other extreme, as we have said, the children of Doña Marina and Doña Luisa were legitimized and ennobled. They were born into a world which their fathers saw as essentially stratified and hierarchical and in which there was a place for them in accordance with the honour due to their parents, a matter in which the qualifying condition was not biology, but belief. But it was a Spanish, not an Indian, hierarchy, based on the Catholic faith, the Spanish language. In general esteem, Spaniards from the peninsula ranked before *criollos*— that is, Spanish born in America—and *criollos* before *mestizos*. But these categories overlapped; the wealthy *mestizo* ranked high above the last needy adventurer from Seville; the heiress to a large *hacienda*, however Indian in appearance, could be confident of a husband from Spain. From this hierarchy, however, the Indian as such was in general excluded; in most regions he could only find a place in it by abandoning his language and his culture.

The Spanish were deeply concerned with precedence and hierarchy and tried to arrange in order and gradation the many combinations of Indian and Spanish blood—a half, a quarter, a sixteenth and many intermediate gradings. There are several series of pictures showing typical examples of these combinations, probably painted by the orders of Spaniards from the peninsula. But the names attached to them suggest many regional variations and it became clear that, as they grew more numerous, the distinctions which these pictures were meant to establish could not really be made in practice. All these types were in fact legally combined in the legal category *las castas*, to which, until the end of the eighteenth century, certain privileges and disabilities were attached.

It is not easy to generalize in so short a summary; there were changes from one period to another and many variations between the regions. At first there was an Indian hierarchy quite separate from the Spanish and to some extent overlapping; there were Indian nobles who were still regarded as Indian. But they became fewer and fewer; in both the Indian empires, the administration had been in the hands of officials of noble birth, not of great hereditary fiefholders, and there was no function for Indian nobles to perform when the Empire had gone. There were variations between the regions, because some were in the hands primarily of ecclesiastical authorities and some of lay, and because there was variation in the proportion of Spanish residents to Indian. But in the broadest terms it can be said that while the Indians have been grossly exploited, have been cheated and discriminated against, they have never been legally defined in a manner from which there could be no escape, while the distinctions made socially have been based at first on religion, later on the community to which a man belonged, biology never being the main determinant.

The generalization can be clarified by contrasting the two cultures which at present exist side by side in Peru. The Inca capital was at Cuzco, high in the Andes at about 13,000 feet above sea level. The Spanish made their capital on the coast, at a new town, now called Lima. This was entirely Spanish and today there is no one in Lima who is called an Indian; when an Indian villager leaves his home in the sierras and goes to seek employment in Lima, it is essential that he should put on clothes of Spanish style, try to speak Spanish and give up characteristic Indian customs such as chewing *coca*. Everyone in Lima is officially supposed to be *mestizo*, part of the money economy, Spanish-speaking and Catholic. But in the sierras there are still four thousand Indian communities, speaking Quechua, living in a subsistence economy, nominally Catholic, but in fact practising many pagan and magical rites, deeply conscious of being despised and usually cheated when they go to the headquarters of their district.[42]

These communities are usually in the higher and least accessible parts of the Andes; in the more open hill country there are *haciendas* where the Indian peons still work on the old system of 180 days' work in the year for the *hacendado*. A beginning is being made with agrarian reform, but the new laws do not apply everywhere and there are obvious means of resisting or postponing their application to a particular estate. About half the population of Peru are generally classed as Indians. It will often happen that an Indian from the *sierras* who has done his spell in the army—and the non-commissioned ranks consist almost entirely of Indians from the *sierras*—will, if he has done well and has acquired some mechanical training, find work in a garage and perhaps eventually end with his own business. But in the process, he will have changed his race. He will now be classed, if he works on the coast, as a *mestizo*. If he went back to the hills and found employment near his original community, he would probably be called a *cholo*, an intermediate category which means an Indian who is beginning to be hispanicized.

But the categories are elastic and have different meanings from one district to the next. They depend also on the outlook of the person who uses them. In one small town in the Andes, it was found that the register of births showed that, for 1927, there were 218 *mestizo* births but no Indian; in 1934, there were 36 *mestizo* and 234 Indian. There had been no change in the population but there had been a change in the town clerk, and the probability is that the clerk of 1934 would have classed his predecessor as an Indian.[43] Pitt-Rivers found groups of whites who referred to everyone but their own small circle as Indian, and, conversely groups of Indians, who referred to everyone but themselves as 'whites', although the neighbours referred to were in fact of Indian appearance.

In Mexico, the capital, Mexico City, was built on the ruins of Tenochtitlan, being at a moderate altitude compared with Cuzco. Partly no doubt for this reason, there is a much less apparent division; the great majority of the population are classed as *mestizo or Iadino*—which means latinized—and it is only in outlying regions that there are still Indian communities speaking an Indian language. Since the Revolution of 1911, it has become fashionable to boast of Indian ancestry and the vast frescoes of the town halls emphasize the nobility of Moteczuma and the Aztecs, the cruelty, greed and brutality of the companions of Cortes; nonetheless, it is still a sign of high social status to look Spanish and the attitude to those who are classified as Indians because they speak an Indian tongue in the home is expressed in the phrase: *Redimir al Indio es integrar la Patria*—to redeem the Indian is to integrate the Fatherland. This is the motto of the Instituto Nacional Indigenista, the government body entrusted with the care of the Indians, and it surely implies that the way to the top is to give up being an Indian.

This highly summarized account will help to explain the concept of Social Race, as expounded by Professor Charles Wagley. Biological Race is little use, in, say, Peru, as a guide to social position; almost everyone has some mixture of Spanish and Amerindian genes. Appearance may be most misleading; I recall one educated young lady, fluent and idiomatic in English as well as Spanish, the daughter of a *hacendado* in the sierras, who, in appearance was pure Amerindian, but who spoke of 'los indios' as hopeless creatures, who would ruin any piece of land with which they were entrusted. They belonged to a different race from her— but a social race, not a biological race. This is a subdivision of the concept for which I suggested the name of Notional Race—which covers the division between nobles and peasants in de Gobineau's thought and in the minds of most characters described by Tolstoy.

There are exceptions in some regions of Latin America to the general rule that, for an Indian, social mobility means racial mobility. One is the north-western part of Guatemala, where the Church was strong and protected the Indians against the loss of their lands. Here there are a certain number of men who have succeeded as doctors, lawyers or merchants and who retain their Indian names, speak the Maya language in the home, and whose wives, if not themselves, will sometimes dress in an Indian style— a trend encouraged by the fact that an embroidered Indian *huipil* is more expensive than a European blouse. Here perhaps is the basis for a regionalism comparable with that of Wales or Brittany. Another exception is Paraguay.

Finally, Negro slaves were brought into the coastal areas of all the Spanish possessions, for much the same reasons as in Brazil and the United States, though never to the same extent. The Negro was stronger than the Indian and more useful as a servant, but he was held in lower esteem. He was not protected by Crown or Church as the Indian was—indeed, Las Casas at one time, though he came to repent it, argued that Negro slaves should be imported in order to preserve the Indians from slavery. It is not very enlightening to say they were not esteemed because they were not protected; why then were they not protected? The Pope had entrusted African territories as well as American to Portugal, and for sixty years, 1580–1640, the Crowns of Spain and Portugal were united. It could not validly be argued that the kingdoms of the West Coast of Africa were less politically advanced than many of the Indian coastal and jungle tribes. It appears to me, as a personal view, that the reason was mainly colour and the associations with colour described in Chapter 4, Section 5.

4 Brazil

Brazil is above all others a country of fluid social definitions, in which there is a continuous scale of racial difference, coinciding to some extent, though by no means exactly, with the social scale. Open discrimination on grounds of race is against the law and provokes strong disapproval in the press. But it would nonetheless be a serious mistake to suppose that race played no part in the social structure.

As has already been said, the Portuguese found in Brazil tribes who were still at a simple food-gathering stage. As in the islands, the American Indians could not be induced to work on plantations and many died because of their lack of immunity to European disease. Negroes were imported; it is estimated that some five million arrived between the beginning of Portuguese government and the end of the trade, in the mid-nineteenth century. Two characteristic institutions developed, the *fazenda* on the coast, the *aldea* inland. The *fazenda* was a plantation, usually specializing in sugar and often called an *engenho* from the engine for crushing sugar-cane, round which production centred. There would be the big house, for the white owner with his family and house-slaves; the slave quarters for the field-slaves, the sugar-cane fields, the plots for the production of food; it was the ideal that the *fazenda* should be as far as possible self-sufficient.

The *aldea* was very different in purpose, organization and composition. This was the mission village, ruled paternally by Portuguese ecclesiastics, whose object was to carry out the task entrusted to the Portuguese by the Pope and to civilize and Christianize the Indians. Indians on the *aldeas* came to be known as *caboclos*, a term usually used with some contempt, with different shades of meaning in different regions, and even in the mouth of the same person at different times, but always implying some degree of Indian origin and some degree of assimilation to Portuguese ways. For a crucial period, the Crowns of Spain and Portugal were united and throughout the whole colonial period there was a similarity of purpose, on the part of both Crown and Church. But there were differences of emphasis, the Crown of Portugul being more concerned with trade and revenue. The religious fraternities who protected the *aldeas* against the encroachments of the *fazendas*, and at some stages against what were virtually slave raids, made themselves very unpopular; indeed, the Jesuits were eventually banished from Brazil for this reason.

Manpower was always short in the Portuguese empire and at several periods there was official encouragement for behaviour for which the Portuguese showed a strong natural inclination. 'Ils aiment la sexe à la folie,' recorded a French visitor and the point seems to have struck everyone who went to Brazil. From the first arrival of the Europeans, the Indian women seem to have accepted their embraces and children to have been born, and there are no signs of the shame and repentance felt by the Dutch at the Cape. There were marriages with baptized Indian women very early, as well as long-standing concubinage. When Negro slaves arrived, children were begotten on slave women. But in marriage distinct preferences were very early established; a girl of mixed Portuguese and Indian blood was preferred to an Indian and a white to either. Marriage with a Negro was very rare in colonial times. Preferences outside marriage were very different.

A pioneer in this field is Dr. Gilberto Freyre; his knowledge is unrivalled and his writing unusually lively and attractive, but his thesis is open to question. He argues that in the great house of the *fazenda*, the family of the owner established with their slaves relationships that might sometimes be cruel but were always warm and personal; they could never be cold and aloof like the Anglo-Saxons. Constant sexual contact provided a warming lubricant to race relations. The Portuguese borrowed from both Negroes and Indians food-stuffs, cookery, dance-steps, hammocks, sandals, and there was thus growing up a new culture compounded from that of each of the three original stocks. Today this view seems very doubtful; it is not much consolation to a man who has lost his fatherland and his freedom to know that his captor imitates his dance-steps and has learnt from him to put pepper in his stew. Nor does it really warm his heart to know that his master makes free with his daughter—unless he can return the compliment. And this was strictly forbidden. There were nine slave rebellions in Bahia between 1807 and 1835, which does not suggest that slavery was popular with the slaves.

But there is no doubt about the mixture of races. There is a verse in a traditional song—one of many which express the same point—which describes the kind of hierarchy that came into existence: 'Whites sleep in beds / Mulattoes in the kitchen / Caboclos on the terrace / Negroes under the hen-roost.' Nor can there be doubt that in colonial Brazil there was strongly-expressed discrimination. The rules for one religious order, for example, insisted on the rejection of any postulant 'proved to be of Moorish, mulatto or Jewish stock or of any other abhorrent race'.[44] One Viceroy would not allow mulatto officers of the militia to enter the room where he sat receiving white officers. An Indian chief in the Eighteenth century was officially degraded for marrying a Negro woman. And there were regiments of militia which confined themselves to white members, others to 'browns' (*pardos*), while some admitted free 'blacks' (*pretos*). It is sometimes argued that the Portuguese in Brazil were free from colour prejudice because they had been accustomed for centuries to being ruled by Muslims who were more civilized than themselves. Quite apart from the fact that neither Arabs nor Berbers are noticeably darker than Portuguese, it is clear from the examples just given that in fact they were prejudiced about ancestry and about colour. But what is significant is that here these deep lines of division blurred and tilted, while in South Africa and the Deep South they grew more rigid; here, it is the case that the father's blood raised a man, not, as in the Deep South, that the mother's conveyed an indelible stain, while there was no general objection to the release of slaves.

It seems in the first place that the Portuguese, to an even greater extent than the Spanish, have been generally proud of their sexual potency rather than ashamed of their incontinence, a point to which we shall return. But there is an economic point of importance also. In the English colonies, there were white artisans and traders who wanted work and resented rivals, while in the Portuguese, even more than in the Spanish territories, no sooner had a man crossed the seas than he esteemed himself a *fidalgo*, whose hands must not be sullied by manual labour. No objection was raised therefore to the common practice of sending from the *fazenda* to the nearest town a slave who had been trained as a wheelwright or shoemaker, hiring him a shop and letting him start a business from which he must remit regular payments to his owner. This also occurred in Cuba. As in Roman law, so in Spanish and Portuguese, a slave could own property, and these *negros de ganha*, as they were called, often saved enough to buy their own freedom. It was expected of an owner that he should free a slave who offered the price for which he had been bought, and eventually it became illegal to refuse. The Church encouraged as an act of charity the release of slaves by will. This marked difference from the English colonies was partly due to the centralized power of Crown and Church, partly to the tradition of Roman law, partly to the lack of artisans eager for work and partly to the general acceptance of a strongly hierarchical social structure. Since there was none of the American egalitarianism, there was no danger

E

in releasing a slave. As a free black, he would know his place in the social structure.

Nonetheless, those freed were at first more often mulatto than black. In 1828, it was calculated that there were 400,000 free mulattoes to 160,000 free blacks. But the proportion of slaves to free was in any case steadily falling; a calculation in 1789 put it at about two slaves to one free black (slaves 1·5 million, free 0·8); by 1872, the proportion was only about one slave to six free. This was partly due to manumission and partly to changing standards of classification, but also to the immigration during the nineteenth century of whites from Europe, of whom about four million are estimated to have arrived between 1820 and 1930.

Thus, instead of a hard line between white and non-white coinciding with a hard line between free and slave, Brazil displays the very different picture of a society in which the first simple division on those lines is quickly diversified into a four-tier society —free white, free mulatto, free black, slave—with the *caboclos* on the fringe, and the jungle Indians altogether outside. The Cape, too, had taken a first step not dissimilar but the direction of social development was there quickly reversed. In Brazil, however, the four categories at once begin to blur and melt into each other because, as in the Spanish territories, and for similar historical reasons, the differences are conceived in religious and cultural rather than biological terms. The gaps fill in to make a continuum and some degree of racial mobility becomes possible. 'Money whitens,' says a Brazilian proverb and another: 'A rich black man is a white and a poor white man is a black.'

But this is true to only a limited extent; although 'white' may in common speech sometimes mean 'rich and successful', there are still strong objections to marriage with people of darker colour. A number of studies have confirmed this, even among university students who are more tolerant than most of the population. This is a matter in which there is a difference between the North and the South of Brazil; Bahia, the old plantation area, where there is a higher proportion of Negroes, conforms outwardly—though not in respect of marriage—much more closely to the Brazilian ideal of no discrimination than the South. In São Paulo, at the other extreme, much covert discrimination is reported. The South is the industrial area and is inevitably the magnet for labour. But when slavery was ended—here not till 1888—the slaves were so unprepared for freedom that some of them thought they need not now go to work unless they wanted. They thus proved poor employees and today find that white immigrants have taken the places in expanding industry which they might have expected.

Brazil was until lately a static society, with a strongly marked hierarchical system which seemed permanent. There was so little movement between classes that there was little need for those high in the scale to put up defences. But with increasing mobility, both social and geographical, with the growth of industry, there seems a danger of increasing rivalry and, in the anonymous world of the industrial city, where parents and kin are not known, it seems likely that physical differences will become increasingly important for identification. In a country which is moving towards a new social structure and where race has been so important an element in the old structure, it is hard to feel confident that Negroes who are newcomers to the industrial scene will get a fair share of employment. Brazil's great asset is public commitment to the idea that racial discrimination is wrong; her great weakness a reluctance to admit that it does take place. Nor does the official doctrine yet recognize the arrogance of its own basic assumption. 'We are becoming one race,' the top Brazilians like to say; they mean of course that certain Negroes who succeed in life are getting more like themselves. But that involves exactly the kind of assumption that white people have made in the United States and which many black people are beginning indignantly to repudiate.

5 The Caribbean

The Caribbean is a term which includes not only many islands, but surrounding mainland territories. Only on the mainland do American Indians survive in any numbers, and even there they are not an important part of the population. Everywhere, there is a history of slave plantations and, in all but some of the smallest islands, most of the population are the descendants of white employers and black slaves.

There is great diversity in the proportions and extent to which these two elements are mixed. In some islands, hardly any residents of unmixed white ancestry remain; in Martinique, it is claimed that no one is wholly black. Here there are *grands blancs, petits blancs, grands mulâtres, petits mulâtres,* and the general mass of the peasantry and landless labourers—five distinct groups between whom there is no intermarriage—and there are gradations within these groups. In some islands, there are little pockets of white peasants who do not appear to have intermarried at all with their black neighbours but who live in an undistinguishable style. In Guyana, Trinidad, and Surinam, the importation of indentured labour from India has produced an element in the population that is physically and culturally unassimilated and which has become a political force of growing importance. But, in spite of these variations, it is possible to speak of a standard Creole structure of society, with a typical history of development; it is possible to regard the society of almost every territory as a variation on this, the East Indians however being outside it. In a summary of this length, the most we can attempt is a sketch of this standard Creole structure, the object being to note how it differs from the developments in Brazil and in the areas of the great pre-Columbian empires.

One of the variable factors in the Caribbean—which from the point of view of the student of race relations is a great natural laboratory—is the nationality of the colonial power; the effect is in some cases somewhat blurred by the fact of the islands having often changed hands. But of this we have spoken elsewhere, and in this section the main emphasis will be on the British islands. In these the system of slavery was similar to that of the Deep South; British metropolitan law took no cognizance of slavery and therefore the slave had none of the protection afforded him by Spanish and Portuguese regulations. This is not to say that there was more or less cruelty in Spanish or British territory; it refers to the legal nature of the institution. The slave could not own property and buy his freedom: it was not the practice in British territories to permit slaves to earn money for their masters and themselves, as in Brazil. In some respects, the operation of the system tended to be harsher in the British West Indies than in Virginia. The owners of estates were often absentees and left it to managers to run their estates for them, demanding only profits. The manager was often trying to save money to buy himself an estate of his own; the field hands suffered. It seems to have been an accepted doctrine in the West Indies that it was better to 'work the slaves out and trust for more supplies from Africa' rather than to prolong their lives by humane treatment. One agent boasted that he had: 'made my employers 20, 30 or 40 more hogsheads of sugar per year than any of my predecessors ever did; and though I have killed 30 or 40 Negroes per year more, yet the produce has been more than adequate to the loss.'[45]

But there was a way of escape. If there was no pressure, as in Brazil, to release slaves, there was none against it, as in Virginia. The children of white masters by slave women in particular were frequently manumitted, sometimes even acknowledged and educated at the father's expense. The moral reasons for this were the opposite of those in Brazil; there the Church was conscious of the inconsistency of slavery with its principles and encouraged manumission. In the British West Indies, until well into the nineteenth century, the Church was corrupt, weak, or non-existent. It exercised no influence against slavery—but also none against incontinence. Men were not ashamed of their offspring. Nor was there economic pressure from white artisans against the release of slaves, as in Virginia. There were few if any white artisans and the society was firmly hierarchical, as in Brazil; there was no feeling that releasing a slave opened the way to a dangerous equality.

Thus, in the most typical situation, we have at first a two-tier organization with a legal basis; free or slave was the distinction. There were indentured white servants as well as black slaves, but increasingly the division between white and black coincided with that between free and slave. Then began a transition to a society organized in three tiers—white slave-owner, free mulatto middle-classes, and artisans; black slaves. And as in Brazil, there was soon a blurring of these lines; some blacks were freed, some mulattoes remained slaves, there were gradations in each tier. There was a counterpoint between racial and social structure, each growing more complex. The shades of colour came to vary from dark brown to parchment; features and hair also revealed ancestry. But actual ancestry was generally known and, in the days before emancipation, legal status remained the first criterion for social position, with colour, hair, and features acting as indications, in a stranger, of a person's legal position, or that of his ancestors and as a means of grading within the two upper tiers.

West Indian societies were distinguished from both Brazil and Virginia by numerical proportions. While in Brazil the proportions at the end of the eighteenth century were two slaves to one free and in Virginia the proportion was nearer four white to one black, in Barbados the proportion of whites was never so high as 10 per cent and in Jamaica it was much less, more like one to twenty. There were three main consequences of this. First, as we have seen, there was no economic opposition to the creation of a middle-class of free coloured; the 'poor white' groups were too small and powerless to protest. The Redlegs of Barbados, for example, the descendants of convicts transported after Monmouth's rebellion (1685), were in no position to resent the release of a slave, still less to express their resentment. Perhaps even more important, their numbers made the whites much more insecure than the slave-owners of Virginia and there must have been some comfort in the presence of a middle class who were unlikely to rise with the slaves and might be expected to side with the whites. Finally, it would have been difficult to keep rigid the kind of distinction made in Virginia between white and non-white, because the coloured were useful to the whites as agents and overseers and in similar capacities.

Once the process of blurring the three tiers had begun, it gathered momentum. There were gradations among the whites, between those from Europe and those born in the Caribbean, and among the latter between those who had some mixture of slave blood and those who had not. Among the middle class, known ancestry and physical appearance as well as education, dress, and wealth indicated social status. Indeed, as time progressed, an outsider might at first have regarded the society as a continuum in which shade of complexion was the most important factor. But in fact what to him appeared a continuum was often a graduated arrangement of in-marrying groups.

Even before emancipation, this blurred three-tier system began to be eroded from the top as neither Brazil nor Virginia were. It was only a man of very moderate ambition who could be contented to stay in the Caribbean; if he had hopes of success in any profession—of fame, of political power—his road lay to Europe. Thus, while the whites in Brazil and Virginia were reinforced by immigrants, from Jamaica there was a continual drain to Europe of the most ambitious, while the larger plantation-owners left things to their agents. After emancipation, this tendency was accentuated; at the same time, the three tiers began to collapse into something much more like two. The whites and mulattoes began to make common cause to exclude the ex-slaves from privilege, and, at the same time, within this one new upper and middle class, there was increasing consciousness of shades of colour as an indication of class and status.

A visitor to the Caribbean will often notice a use of language which is puzzling and for which the explanation given is frequently misleading. He will hear someone of dark complexion and African features referred to as a white man, sometimes by those who regard him as a social superior, sometimes by himself. And if he asks about this he will be told by anyone from the upper tiers that this is because in the Caribbean there is so little race consciousness; it is a strongly differentiated class system, he will be told, and 'white' simply means upper-class—it is merely a historical survival. What is true in this explanation is that words with a physical meaning such as 'black' and 'white' are used in the Caribbean in a social rather than a biological sense; what is misleading is to suggest that this is due to a lack of racial consciousness. On the contrary the sense of a racial hierarchy is so strong that it overrides other considerations. White means rich and black means poor, no matter what the message of one's eyes.

In this respect, the Caribbean is the most colonial of all societies. What is most disliked about colonialism is that the few impose on the many a spiritual yoke which governs their actions and thoughts more pervasively even than the physical force which lies in the background. This was achieved more thoroughly in the Caribbean than anywhere else—more even than in Brazil—because the slaves were torn completely away from their own culture and deliberately mixed—as they were not in Brazil—so that people who spoke the same language should not stay together. They lost language, memories, customs, religion; they were brought up in ignorance of any tradition except the one fact they could observe, that to be white was to be rich, comfortable and free.

This produced an inescapable dilemma—central to an understanding of race relations—more poignant in the Caribbean than anywhere else. This man, the former slave, who is black, looks at his employer, once his owner, who is white and free and rich; he looks with envy and desire—this is what he wants to be. But the white man is the obstacle in his path and must be hated as well as admired. And who is he, the black man? 'Stop acting like a nigger,' his mother used to tell him.[46] Then how is he to act? Like a white man? But that means he must behave arrogantly and contemptuously towards *himself*. And, in extreme cases, this self-contempt takes the form of regarding himself as an exception; in spite of the evidence of his looking-glass, he himself is really white, not at all like his friends.

Here in the Caribbean was far less resignation to the lot of the slave than in Virginia. Perhaps this was because of the numerical relationship, also because of the possibility of release; the situation was less hopeless. There were many slave risings. Today the quest for an identity, a cultural pedigree, is fiercer here than anywhere. Here arose many strange religious cults, seeking escape from an intolerable present, often in myths of an Ethiopian past and a return one day to a glorious and romantic Africa. West Indians have been the leaders of many such movements in the United States. Here arose the much more sophisticated concept of 'négritude'; but, as an African acutely remarked, 'a tiger does not go about proclaiming its tigritude; it just pounces.'[47] West Indians cannot feel that they are African; being black would be irrelevant to their needs, if only it were also irrelevant in the eyes of the whites whom they have been so painfully taught to admire, emulate, and dislike.

Meanwhile, most of the Caribbean territories are seriously over-crowded. There is a very great discrepancy between the incomes of the few rich and the majority; there is both unemployment and under-employment among the lower class, the black descendants of the slaves. There are virtually two cultures, two sets of values. The light-coloured middle classes in the English-speaking islands admire the Victorian middle classes, the virtues of thrift and fore-thought, the institutions of property and marriage; the dark lower classes may sometimes express similar attitudes, but if so they are held, simultaneously and ambivalently, with a quite different set of beliefs on which action is more frequently based. These include a folk religion with magical and pre-Christian elements; an attitude to marriage and the family, a hostility to law and the police, which go back to slavery. And the outward signs of the two cultures are still shades of complexion. West Indians of the middle classes, particularly from Jamaica, will sometimes speak of 'brown' and 'black' as though these were two utterly different nationalities, and will unhesitatingly allot to these categories people between whose colouring an outsider would hardly distinguish.

In the past, it was an overwhelming advantage to be light-coloured; it was easier to get a job, particularly if it meant dealing with the public; it meant being served first in a shop and in a dozen ways treated with deference and respect. Since independence and the extension of the franchise, this begins to change. In politics, it *has* changed; it is easier for a dark man to get votes. 'A brown man like myself could hardly get a hearing in that constituency,' a prominent politician told me. For a time it seemed as though, at least in some islands, there might be a division of power, political leadership going to the black majority and their representatives, while control of private enterprise remained with whites and the light-coloured. But this honeymoon seems unlikely to last indefinitely; the pressure at elections is bound to increase and the obvious targets for attack are expatriate businesses and large plantations.

There are a number of elements outside the standard Creole structure. The most important group are the East Indians who came as indentured labourers to replace the slaves and who on the whole have remained culturally and physically distinct. East Indians and Creoles each have derogatory mental pictures of each other; the Creole to the Indian seems idle, spendthrift, and promiscuous; the Indian to the Creole cunning, miserly, humourless, clannish, and liable to cheat his simpler neighbour. In Guyana, the Indians would, on the usual British voting system, have a majority of the votes, and voting has increasingly followed racial lines. But they have been for the moment kept out of power by a system of voting adopted in no other former British territory. In Trinidad, where they are not yet in a majority, they are offered a share in the Government and the ruling party provided they will give up their cultural diversity—or in other words become Creolized. It is safe to say that by neither of these methods is harmony likely to be achieved.

The Portuguese, Jews, Syrians, and Chinese, who are present in various proportions in several territories, face a common dilemma. They have in the past frequently succeeded in business and have usually identified themselves with light-coloured Creole society by all means short of marriage, and sometimes also by marriage. Today this is to their disadvantage; in the language of the Caribbean, they are white, and the descendants of the slaves have learnt to look on whites as people who have all the good there is but from whom no good is to be expected. It would be surprising if they did not become targets for hostility. The Caribbean territories are generally overpopulated and the goods they are best fitted to supply to the world are in too great supply. They are too small to build up sizeable internal markets and have refused the road of federation; the dilemmas which face them seem inescapable. And in such circumstances, minorities are liable to suffer.

6 India, West Africa, New Zealand

In the present section, it will be possible only to sketch, in respect of three societies, just enough to make the general argument in the next chapter intelligible. I must reluctantly say nothing about the Indian caste system, a most complex social structure embodying a number of racial myths, which was held together by the belief that it was divinely ordained. But it is necessary to refer to the British in India, because of the contrasts they present to the Spanish in America, and indeed to most other imperial systems.

As has already been said, the British went to the court of the Mughal Emperor at the beginning of the seventeenth century as suppliants for trade; it was a more powerful empire than the Peruvian, and based on a civilization which had used writing for many than two thousand years, but it was an empire at a similar stage of development to the Incas' and, under the great Akbar,* had approached the efficiency and foresight ascribed to the Incas. But it deteriorated in the hands of emperors who did not, as Akbar had done, give thought to preserving for the peasant a share of the crop sufficient to keep him at work and at least prevent him from deserting his holding. Nonetheless, it was a century and a half before, in 1758, the British took effective power into their hands, and even then it was indirectly by installing a puppet as fiefholder of the Emperor in one province, Bengal. There was conflict, from the middle of the eighteenth century, between the expansionists, usually in India, and those fearful of political entanglements, usually in London; French rivalry, the difficulty of doing business in a society that was becoming steadily more chaotic, the advantage held by the man on the spot when letters may take a year to reach him—all these were on the side of the expansionists.

The expansion began in earnest when Wellesley was Governor

---

* The first British ambassador carried letters addressed to Akbar Shah, but he had died in 1605 and his son was on the throne before they were delivered.

General, two hundred years after the arrival of the first ambassador; Pizarro had killed Atahualpa and made himself master of Peru in the year after he landed. Thus the intention and pace could hardly have been more different from the Spanish. And, by the time of Wellesley, a number of decisions had been taken which were to last for the remaining century and a half of British rule. It had already been decided not to interfere with the religion of the inhabitants of the country, to keep very small the number of British officials, to choose them carefully, give them adequate training and pay them well. Artisans and manual workers were never imported in any numbers; the officials were expected to return to England when they retired, and usually did. The number of British in India, including troops, did not usually exceed a proportion of about one to three thousand of the native population. The British officials were less than one to sixty thousand.

In all these respects, the British empire in India was quite different from anything in America, or in those parts of Africa where there were white settlers who meant to stay permanently. The officials, and the comparatively few planters and businessmen remained aloof from the native inhabitants; there was, in the classical period, a line of demarcation between British and Indian. But it was a tilted line and a Maharaja might employ a British secretary, while after 1919, British officials were often under the orders of Indians. Disengagement was easy in comparison with Algeria or Rhodesia; to retire to England earlier than one had meant is not comparable with the shock of uprooting from the country of one's birth. During the last thirty years of British rule, half the officials of the highest services were Indian, there were elected provincial and central assemblies, there were the elements of a democratic system of local government, preparations were being made for a handover. Whatever doubts Indians had about British good faith, whatever anger at continued paternalism, whatever disputes about pace, this was clearly something quite different from South Africa, where the whites are permanently settled, believe that they have nowhere else to go, and have no intention of sharing power or handing it over.

There is one further point to be made. During the classical period of British rule, British officials and military officers were aloof in all respects, even from Indian women: any entanglement was unusual and had to be clandestine. Marriage was virtually unknown. The case was different with soldiers not of commissioned rank, but their encounters with Indian women were with prostitutes and for them, too, marriage was rare. In the beginning of British rule, things were different and it was common for officers to keep 'female servants', usually for purely physical purposes, but marriage, and even long concubinage, though it occurred, was infrequent. This was quite different from Burma, although at one time Burma was a province of the Indian Empire; here, marriage with Burmese wives was never frowned on and throughout it was fairly common practice for a district officer or judge to live in happy companionship with a local Burmese girl for so long as he stayed in the district; when he was transferred, they seem usually to have parted amicably and the girl married without reproach. This difference between Burma and India is clearly due to the Indian caste system; no high-caste Indian girl could marry outside her own group. But the change in British attitudes reflects a change in British society. And in the last stage of British rule, something unusual occurred. Mixed marriages became respectable, and indeed rather fashionable, but liaisons outside marriage were still almost unknown.

West Africa is mentioned here only for the contrast it affords with South Africa. Its climate, and the very high incidence of yellow fever and forms of malaria often fatal to Europeans, are one factor in the situation; another is the presence of primitive states considerably better organized than any met by the Afrikaners in their first contacts. The Portuguese, Dutch, and English in turn built forts along the coast to protect the goods which they assembled to wait for ships; they negotiated with chiefs who would supply the goods they wanted, often slaves; it was common, when a ship came in, for its captain to spend a preliminary day or two in feasting and drinking with the chiefs with whom he would eventually do business. By the end of the nineteenth century, no local state was strong enough to resist the coming of Europeans, but the terms on which they met continued to follow the old pattern, while the climate ensured that once political rule had been secured, officials and business men would follow the Indian pattern and retire to Britain. Thus in British possessions in West Africa, relations were in many respects more like those in India than those in South Africa. But, as in Burma, there was no caste system, and concubinage occurred, as it did not in India.

New Zealand belongs to quite a different category. The Maoris were a stone-age Polynesian people when Europeans first encountered them. They had been in New Zealand for a few centuries only, having come by sea, and were loosely organized in tribes and clans. They had no primitive state comparable with Benin or Ba-Rotseland, but on the other hand they were more advanced than the Hottentots and impressed Europeans by their physical beauty and by their decorative arts. Early travellers describe a people who put a high value on the kind of virtues admired by Homer or by a Scottish Highland Chief in the eighteenth century—courage, hospitality, loyalty to friend and kinsman, generosity, a strong sense of personal honour. It was easy for Europeans in the eighteenth century to believe that they had found the Noble Savage. But this image was soon marred; there were reports of cannibalism and what to the Europeans seemed treachery, though to the Maoris it would often be the defence of something sacred which was perhaps unwittingly threatened. A double image of the Maori has persisted, perhaps more strongly than in the case of any other subordinate group; the Pakeha—the Maori word for a European—even today will sometimes speak of the 'real' or 'unspoilt' Maori who is gay, brave, childlike, artistic, fond of song, but will contrast him with the town Maori who is idle, improvident, given to drink, promiscuous.

Contact began towards the end of the eighteenth century. At first, Maoris took readily to what was useful in the new culture and used it for their own purposes; they saw that steel was better than stone and used it for their carvings without changing the patterns. But soon the penetration of different customs began to be more significant; missionaries established mission stations, traders set up stores, Maoris engaged themselves to serve as hands on long sea voyages. Land began to be alienated to Europeans—there was still plenty; Maoris took enthusiastically to Christianity and to many more tangible accompaniments, to growing wheat and grinding it in mills, to ploughs, carts, cattle, and horses. But their land grew less and less; the Treaty of Waitangi in 1840 transferred sovereignty—a concept the Maoris cannot entirely have understood—to Queen Victoria and vested in the Crown all unoccupied land. But much land, which to Pakehas seemed unoccupied, had been important to the Maoris; they saw it 'developed' and it was lost to them.

The Treaty had acknowledged as Maori reserves over twenty-eight million acres in the North Island and thirty-eight million in the South; by 1891, these had shrunk to a quarter million only in the South Island and less than eleven million in the North. Four-fifths had gone. At the same time, less tangibly, all the concepts that held their society together had been destroyed; by accepting Christianity they shattered a system of belief based on the sacredness of certain people, parts of the body, trees, plants, degrees of kinship, and age. Nothing took the place for the Maoris of this system of respect, which served to hold the society together: as Christians, they became socially white men who were not really white.

There came a period of active rebellion against the new white society, the 'King' movement, the Hau-Hau movement, a series of campaigns in which the Maoris were defeated, though not crushed: then followed a period of withdrawal. The Government continued a policy of encouraging individual land-holdings which encroached still further on communal lands; Maoris were represented in Parliament; Pakehas said that they had solved the race problem, there was no colour bar and no discrimination, but would add, if questioned, that the Maoris were a dying race. It was thought that there had once been a quarter of a million, but in the last years of the nineteenth century there were only about 40,000 and it was believed that they were doomed. But by the twenties of the present century, numbers were rising and the forecast for 1975 is that they will be back at a quarter of a million.

Thus the acute loss of confidence and of will to live has passed. But it is far from true that there is no Maori problem. In a competitive and individualist society, there is a visibly different minority of whom the majority have two inconsistent stereotypes; one is a vision of the Noble Savage brought up to date and has little reality, the other, of the Maori as he is today, is just the picture which successful middle-class people in a competitive society do have of those who are unsuccessful. Of course, there are exceptions, Maoris who have made good in Parliament and in the professions, but they have achieved success at the expense of their *Maori-tanga* —their Maori-hood, their *négritude*, their *indigénismo*. That all these concepts, in the form in which they have been revived, are slightly bogus does not alter the reality, as pictured by James Ritchie, of the dilemma which faces the Maori boy in the centre of the North Island when he goes to school. His teachers expect him to have language difficulties and difficulties at home because his parents may be barely literate and do not understand the need for homework; they expect that he will be an early leaver and drift into the lowest grade of employment in forestry or casual farm employment. All this usually proves to be true. He *may* make good in school in spite of this but the more successful he is, the more he will be alienated from his parents without being fully accepted into the white society.

This picture would be contested; in the South Island the Maori is more likely to be urban, and at school his situation is much that of the child in any great town who comes from the lowest ranks of the unskilled and whose parents are barely literate. He is, however, marked as different by his appearance, and, although there is no colour bar, there is a clearly marked scale of relationships in which he becomes progressively less acceptable. He is all right, said one Pakeha, to work with or to have a drink with, but not as a neighbour, still less as a relation by marriage.[48] Nonetheless, mixed marriages do occur and, although the relations on both sides usually object and prophesy dire results, they are often amenable to reason and sometimes withdraw their objections when they meet the new relation and come to appreciate his qualities or hers. It is on the whole a fluid and tolerant society, very different from South Africa. Here, after all, it is not the dominant group who are afraid of losing their identity.

7 Britain

In the other sections of this chapter, we have been considering situations which, after varying periods of flux, settled down to a recognizable structure, to which there were no doubt exceptions and qualifications but which, in general, was for a time fairly static. Britain is different because the problem is a new one and the period of flux has only just begun; the immigration is very recent and in itself small, but it has accentuated some existing problems in British society, particularly in respect of housing, education, and employment, and has occurred at a time of acute social and political readjustment.

Thus the situation is utterly different from any of the others at which we have looked. The immigrants, though no doubt impelled by economic forces, have come of their own choice; they are a small minority, even taken together, but in fact there are three main elements, very different in outlook and background; they have come to an industrial and competitive society, more developed in this respect than their own, a society whose professed ideals are hostile to a settled system of domination and subordination by race. There are some parallels with race relations in the American North, few with the South; there are also some with New Zealand, in spite of the fact that in that country the minority belonged to a stone-age culture and preceded the Europeans.

An essential aspect of the British situation is that the island has not been invaded by foreign conquerors for nine hundred years. Before that, a succession of invasions had mixed a number of different populations, but the differences between the genetic stocks that made up the mixture were comparatively slight; in neither a physical nor cultural sense would the shock of contact, at least since Anglo-Saxon times, compare with the arrival of Cortes in Mexico or van Diemen in the South Pacific. Even the Norman Conquest, though brutal and sudden, was achieved by a people physically little different from the English, of the same religion, and technically and socially only slightly ahead of them. This long period without any massive influx of population imposed from above has given the inhabitants of the island a strong sense of their own homogeneity and a corresponding distrust of foreigners. There have, from time to time, been small immigrations, Flemish refugees from religious persecution in the sixteenth century, Huguenots in the seventeenth, Russian Jews at the end of the nineteenth. To all these the reaction was similar; at the official level, there were good political reasons for welcoming the Flemings, and they also brought valuable skills in weaving—but English weavers were less pleased than their employers and sometimes turned on the Flemish with violence. It was the same with Huguenots and Russian Jews—official tolerance was faced with popular disapproval. In the case of the Jews, fleeing from pogroms encouraged by the Tsar's officials, popular agitation in Britain led to the Aliens Act, which for the first time imposed restrictions on the entry of foreigners to Britain.

Of a special character was the Irish influx from the mid-nineteenth century onwards. There was seldom a fixed intention of staying, rather of earning good money for unskilled work and taking it back; some of the influx was purely seasonal, for hay-making and harvest through June, July and August, but in fact many drifted from job to job, failed to save and stayed on. The Irish navvies who dug the canals, laid the railway tracks, and made the macadam roads of Victorian England had not the skills of the Jews and Huguenots; they were despised and disliked by the English as dirty, improvident, drunken and violent, and the familiar machinery of the self-fulfilling prophecy made it difficult for them to escape from the pool of unskilled labour. In Victorian literature, the references to them often recall the language used of the American Negro in the North. But they were not black, and it was not difficult to go back across the Irish Sea.

We have spoken already of the contradiction at the heart of an imperial democracy. The arrival of the Jewish refugees from Russia revealed another aspect of this contradiction; throughout the century, Britain had given moral support to Greek, Hungarian, Italian nationalists; just as the France of Louis XVI had supported the rebellion of the American colonies, so Britain had supported the Spanish colonies in their wars of independence. Kossuth, Marx, Mazzini, and many more had found exile in Britain from foreign despotism. And there had been pride in the liberalism, the tolerance, exercised at the expense of the Tsar and the Emperor of Austria. It was another matter when, instead of a few intellectuals, thousands of Jews speaking Russian, Polish or Yiddish, came to settle in Leeds or the East End of London. It was said that they brought disease, that they threatened British ethical and cultural standards; the Aliens Act was passed as a temporary measure and became permanent.

In varying degrees, these different elements became part of the British social structure. This appeared to an outsider as a continuum, though with a great range of difference, in wealth, power and esteem, between the two ends, between a Duke of Omnium and an Irish navvy. This was so far true that there were fewer rigid distinctions than in pre-revolutionary Europe; there was no legally defined noble caste, the younger sons of a peer being commoners, but in fact the society was much more stratified and the distinctions were much sharper than appeared from outside. 'How is it that there are no tradesmen's sons at Eton or Harrow? There is no law, written or unwritten which excludes them . . . yet the boys take good care that if one comes, he shall not stay . . .'

wrote G. O. Trevelyan, the biographer of Macaulay.[49] The whole
society, from the unskilled labourer upward, was pervaded by
gradations that were never defined in law, but perfectly clear to
those whom they concerned. They might be modified, though not
in one or even two generations obliterated, by personal success.
'Were she an heiress, the world would forgive her birth on account
of her wealth,' wrote Trollope in *Dr. Thorne*, and the theme of
marriage between men and women at subtly different levels in the
gradation of esteem, of how far money can atone for the lack of
'blood'—or 'blood' for lack of money—is recurrent throughout the
nineteenth century. This was not only in the higher ranks; a
farmer's daughter must not marry a tradesman, nor an artisan's
an unskilled labourer. In Brazil or Mexico, the calculations would
take into account a third dimension, not only wealth and known
ancestry but racial ancestry as revealed by appearance. 'Money
whitens', just as money makes up for birth. This element was
virtually absent in Britain until the twentieth century.*

The 'premise of inequality' was thus strong in British society
until 1914. But there was some awareness of the contradictions it
implied; a theme in *Punch* is the obsequiousness to a lord of the
free-born Englishman, whose home is his castle; Magna Carta was
supposed to have guaranteed equality before the law, the principles of the Declaration of Rights logically implied an extension
of political power which did in fact take place during the century.
The Wars of 1914 and 1939 accelerated the process of broadening
both the economic and the social bases of society. The concept of
the Welfare State was thought, in the early fifties, to be leading
towards a classless society. To the disruption of social convention
involved in much genuine reform and in the professed rejection
of the old 'premise of inequality' was added the even more disrup-
tive element of disillusion because class differences in fact persisted.
On top of this came the loss of empire. Naval and maritime
supremacy had vanished, together with an empire which had
included a fifth of the world's population.

For a brief period it was believed that the Empire would be
replaced by a Commonwealth of independent nations, held together not by metropolitan power, but by common ideals. But, as
the new nations of the Commonwealth fumbled for their nation-

---

* Virtually, but not quite. See George Sedley's objections to marrying Miss
Schwarz, the West Indian heiress, in *Vanity Fair*.

hood, seeking some bond of unity that would replace imperial power, it became increasingly clear that they would follow their own lines of political development internally, seek trade and finance wherever they could find them, and make alliances in which British apron-strings would play no part. By the late sixties, a mood of disillusion with the idea of the Commonwealth prevailed and it was exactly true, as an American observer remarked, that Britain had lost an empire but not yet found a role. In the population of such a state, there was bound to be an element which had once gloried in the feeling of superiority bestowed by imperial rule, which now felt defrauded, which was particularly ready to make a scapegoat of the former subjects of the Empire, which was resentful at their intrusion into the homogeneous nation-state.

The immigration of the post-war years was due to British reluctance to define by rule any situation which was not openly giving trouble, more directly to the optimism which veiled the discrepancy between ideals and fact about the Commonwealth. It was possible for citizens of the British Caribbean territories, of India and of Pakistan, to enter Britain on a passport issued by their own government without any restriction and thereupon at once to enjoy the rights of British citizens, to stay permanently, to vote and to receive the benefits and pay the taxes and contributions of the Welfare State. Since average incomes in Jamaica were less than a sixth and in India less than a twentieth of those in Britain, what is surprising is that the immigration did not start sooner; in fact, the first tiny trickle from the Caribbean did not reach 1,000 a year until 1951, nor 10,000 a year until 1954, but rose to 30,000 in 1956 and 60,000 in 1961. Neither Indian nor Pakistani immigration reached 10,000 a year till 1961. In 1962, a control on entry came into force and the inflow dropped sharply; by 1964, it was estimated that the total number of 'coloured' persons in Britain was less than one million, or 2 per cent of the population.

Before the fifties, there had been a few thousand coloured seamen in the seaports, Cardiff, London, Liverpool; and scattered throughout the country a few hundred Indians, some of whom were professional men, for the most part doctors, while some were itinerant pedlars. British authorities ignored their origin; they were not officially distinguished from the rest of the population. But with growing numbers, colour made newcomers a target for resentment; it was inevitable that they should cluster, as all immigrants do, where their friends had settled and where work was available. Thus colour made them conspicuous. Perhaps the tolerance which the British believed themselves to possess might have extended further had the immigration occurred at the height of their self-confidence and before the social changes just sketched.

The differences between the three groups must be emphasized. About a half was from the Caribbean: we have already mentioned the ambivalence of the Caribbean peasantry, and all the evidence suggests that, in those who save or borrowed money for the journey to Britain, what was uppermost was the determination to be 'white', that is to say to adopt Victorian, middle-class values. Nonetheless, to the British, profoundly ignorant of Caribbean history and geography, they often seemed flamboyant and alien. There was a far deeper cultural difference in the case of the Indians and Pakistanis; language, religion, clothes, and food were foreign to the inhabitants of the island.

It is not the purpose of this section to attempt to describe the course of events in Britain, only to indicate how different the situation is from others we have looked at. It is necessary however to say that agitation against the unrestricted entry of *coloured* immigrants grew in intensity during the late fifties, as it had in respect of Jews at the beginning of the century.[50] It had not been so intense immediately after the War in respect of Poles and other Europeans, partly no doubt because their entry was controlled. They had differed from the native inhabitants in language and religion, and in many customs; their colour however permitted them to fit into the native scene. One government introduced controls on immigration in 1962 and three years later its successors —who had opposed their introduction—continued and intensified them. In each of the two main parties there was by 1965 a central group whose views on the control of immigration and on race relations were not dissimilar; both believed that, in order to prevent friction, it was necessary to control the number of visibly different persons who entered the country and thus obtained the right to stay permanently; they also believed that those in the country should be treated in the same way as other citizens— though the parties differed as to how this could be done.

Much confusion was caused by the fact that aliens from Europe were admitted without restriction on numbers, but with restrictions on civil rights and on the right to stay, while Commonwealth citizens were restricted in numbers but not in other respects. Still more anomalous was the position of the Irish, whose country had left the Commonwealth but who were admitted without restriction either of numbers or citizenship. These distinctions made the coloured Commonwealth immigrants to Britain feel themselves the victims of discrimination; at the same time, the restrictions placed on their admission also affected the entry of white Australians and Canadians, whom no one supposed likely to cause friction. Reluctance to clean the slate and make a fresh start over immigration on a more logical basis thus hampered the attempts of the government to improve relations within the country; nonetheless a start was made with legislation against discrimination and it was later extended in scope.

In both parties there were minority groups whose views were dissimilar from those of their party leaders and sharply opposed to each other's. As in the case of earlier immigrations to Britain, there was probably a greater tolerance among the official classes than among the general population; probably a large proportion of the population would have preferred the country to stay as far as possible homogeneous, while on the other hand many were uneasy at proposals which were manifestly unjust or discriminatory against those who had been legally admitted. But as the debate proceeded it became increasingly clear that the emotional issue was *colour*; agitation was not directed against the admission of Irish or continental aliens. In the fifties, the very few sociologists who had studied the question had included some who believed that what appeared to be race prejudice in Britain was a form of class prejudice, while others thought that the most part of the population regarded the coloured man as the 'archetypal stranger'. By the late sixties, neither of these views was tenable as more than a partial explanation of what was happening; I have already argued that there were historical grounds for regarding them as insufficient even before the immigration.

Thus Britain at the turn of the decade from the 1960's to the 1970's is in the midst of a debate; all attitudes are still fluid, the situation is still new. It cannot seriously be doubted that immigrants of colour have sometimes met hostility, have often found it difficult to get lodgings or jobs; it has been argued that this is due not to colour, but to differences of behaviour and beliefs. The fate of those who seek employment after full schooling in Britain will illuminate this point. So far Governments have vacillated between professed ideals and fear of the electorate; there has been no firm historical decision such as we have seen taken, in opposite senses, in Spain in the sixteenth century and South Africa in the twentieth. There is still room for leadership, time for such a decision; whether it will be taken remains to be seen.

8
Disentangling the Causes

---

1 Numbers

THE purpose of this chapter is to consider certain factors in the situations we looked at in the last chapter and in a few others which there has not been room to describe. How far have these factors affected the development of race relations in these territories? Have any of them been in any sense decisive?

The first factor to be examined is the numerical proportions of the groups concerned. The method is first to make a broad classification of various types of situation, which seems to arise from the descriptions in the last chapter and then to apply to that classification this one factor of numbers. Some interesting patterns emerge.

The classification is under four heads. We can for this purpose ignore one kind of relationship, now obsolete, the 'plural societies' described by Furnivall, in which a number of communities lived together amicably under a strong imperial rule. The aftermath of this situation is to be seen in Malaya, in Trinidad, Guyana, Mauritius, and Fiji; all these are situations still undecided, in which contending parties have as yet reached no balance. If these are omitted, the four main classes of relationship between ethnically distinct groups in one state are: Dominant, Paternalist, Competitive, and Fluid as to Racial Definition.

The supreme example of a dominant society at present is South Africa; here one group has a monopoly of political power, and enormous advantages in wealth, education, esteem, and opportunity. It has no intention of sharing these advantages with the subordinate group. Rhodesia is not very different in this respect, nor was the Deep South. In the ancient world, Sparta established a similar kind of society, in three tiers: in Africa before the coming of Europeans, the Tutsi were dominant over the Hutu in Ruanda in much the same way, and there is another example to which we have not previously referred, the Brahman monopoly of land ownership, wealth, education, power, and ritual prestige, which was typical of many villages in Southern India fifty years ago. The Brahmans were a congeries of in-marrying groups who conceived of themselves as of a different racial origin from their tenants and the untouchables. There was a similar system, with Rajputs in place of Brahmans, in many parts of Northern India. But there was no legal enforcement of these restrictions and they had no sanction at the level of what is now the State or the Federal Union. In all these examples we can see a monopoly of privilege and no intention of parting with it.

There is another group of societies in which a different intention is proclaimed and does to some extent influence behaviour, though it is seldom carried out in full. The British in India early in the nineteenth century decided that the justification for their presence was 'the improvement of the natives' and foresaw a day when this would have reached a stage when they would no longer be required; it is true that this was at a point in the remote future and that it was frequently forgotten, even by men in high position, but the ideal remained and from 1919 onwards preparations were being made to leave. The concept of trusteeship again applied in the British colonial territories in Africa, though the time scale was imagined as even more prolonged. The French aims, first of assimilation and later of association, were in many ways very different but, like the British, contemplated a change in the relationship as the assimilation became more complete. These relationships, which were ostensibly of trusteeship, I would class as Paternalist; there are obviously border-line cases between paternalism and dominance, and sometimes one changes into the other; one might call the Crown of Spain's attitude to the Indians in America paternalist but the first republican governments were dominant. The key lies in the difference between the Latin meaning of the words; paternalism is the relationship of a father to a son, who will one day be independent; it is intended to benefit the son and the relationship can be healthy unless it is prolonged after the son comes of age. Dominance on the other hand is the relationship of master to servant or slave; it is frankly for the benefit of the master and is permanent. Despite difficulties of definition, and the element of hyprocrisy so often present in paternalism, the distinction seems to me a real one, clearly marked in the extreme cases, the British in India and the present society in South Africa.

The third classification is Competitive and here the examples are the northern cities of America, Great Britain, and New Zealand, which resemble each other in that a minority (or in Britain minorities) wish, on the whole, to obtain a place in a competitive industrial society and are prevented from complete success, not by regulation but by lack of training, opportunity, and incentive; by varying forms of discrimination, sometimes by parental upbringing. Finally, there are the societies of Fluid Racial Definition, where race is only one of the factors used in assessing social status and where one man may be described by different racial terms at different stages of his life, or in accordance with the social position, or even the momentary mood, of the speaker. These include the Caribbean territories, Brazil, and the Spanish-speaking territories in Central America and the Andes.

In the first table, which follows immediately, I have hesitated to include the Fluid societies because, my definition, it is not easy to say what exactly are the proportions within a shifting continuum. But a very rough division between an upper and lower group can be made. Nor is the third column very revealing, because the definition of this category of society indicates that the lower group is a minority. But the first two columns are interesting; the classification was made on the basis of the attitudes of the dominant group and the numerical proportions were not taken into account, but they fall within a very clear range.

A dominant minority is clearly in a stronger position if it has modern weapons which it can deny to the majority, if it has a competent intelligence service and police force and if it is prepared to be ruthless. The nature of the country, and whether it is suitable for guerrilla operations, will also make a difference. In all these respects the South African government is in a stronger position than the numbers of the upper group suggest. But, though these factors will vary the proportions, it seems from these examples that the establishment of a frank and permanent dominance by a racial minority can only occur within a certain range of numerical proportion. Rhodesia was a border-line case and, without South

TABLE 1

Table showing approximate numerical proportions between
Superordinate and Subordinate Groups in four Categories of
Society

Dominant	Paternal	Competitive	Fluid (very approx.)
South Africa: 1–4	British India: 1–3000	U.S.A. 1960 (Northern): 15–1	Brazil 1–2
Rhodesia: 1–16	Nigeria 1952: 1–2000	U.K. 1968: 50–1	Jamaica: 1–20
Deep South: 4–1	Nyasaland: 1–1060 1945 1–520 1966	New Zealand: 13–1	Mexico: 10–1
Tutsi in Ruanda: 1–6	Uganda: 1–650		Peru: 1–1
Brahman Village (three-tier): 1 : 2 : 1	Tanganyika: 1–450		
Sparta (three-tier): 1 : 1 : 2	Kenya: 1–100		

African support, might well have been by now on the way to
African rule. Kenya was also a border case and would at one time
have been classed as dominant, but the white minority depended
on support from Britain and crumpled as soon as this was withdrawn. It is interesting that a recent American writer[51] classifies
Uganda, Tanganyika and Kenya, when they were colonial territories, in that order in respect of the degree to which native
interests were consulted; it is in reverse order to the proportion
of whites. The number of whites is of course partly due to the
climate, which also affects their attitude to change; where they
think of themselves as permanent inhabitants, they want to run
the country for their own benefit. But they cannot achieve this
unless they reach certain proportions.

It has been argued, with vigour and dogmatically, by Marvin
Harris[52] that numbers alone are enough to explain the contrast
between the fluidity of Brazilian society and the rigidity of the

rule, in the Deep South, that the least element of non-white blood makes a man a Negro. (He does not say that numbers *are* the only reason but that they would be sufficient by themselves.) I have already suggested reasons for thinking that the determining factors are more complicated. But on numbers alone the argument falls to the ground if one includes some other societies besides Brazil and the Deep South. It becomes, of course, progressively more difficult in Brazil to give firm figures for a distinction which is not openly made, but we have seen that, in colonial times, the population was estimated at one free to two slave, while the white population was believed to be 24 per cent of the population in 1835; 38 per cent in 1872; 44 per cent in 1941. For the purpose of comparison with the Deep South's four to one, it may be taken as one to two. But, if this were the overriding factor that Harris would have us believe, the Deep South would be the most rigid of the former slave societies, Brazil next and South Africa third. In fact, of course, while numbers put Brazil in a class with South Africa and the Deep South, on the basis of social structure it must be classed with Jamaica, where the proportion was usually more in the neighbourhood of one to twenty. Numerical proportion has little to do with fluidity, but does have a relationship to rigidity.

Numerical proportion must not, therefore, be looked on as a sole determining factor. But it may be a limiting factor for societies which 'decide'—it is not necessarily a conscious decision taken at a specific moment—on permanent dominance. And numerical proportion also plays a part in the competitive type of society, though again one must beware of attempting to fix any exact proportion at which certain results will follow. If a minority is so small that it is not seen as a threat it will not be resented; a stage may however come when increasing numbers give the minority a greater confidence, which to the majority may seem aggressive. The majority may now feel that its homogeneity is threatened, and, indeed, that the identity of the community is being changed. At this stage developments will depend on the leadership on both sides; numbers which cause acute anxiety in one community will give no offence in another. But there is a fairly wide belt of proportions where the initiative rests with the majority. Here the minority have no sensible alternative but to plead—no doubt also to remonstrate at unfairness—but basically to acquiesce in a situation, to which they must accommodate themselves as best they can. But, if their numbers reach a pitch where they can make themselves felt politically, more vigorous tactics are open to them. The judgment as to when the right moment for this has come will depend on their assessment of the majority, its ideals, its leadership, the degree of hostility likely to develop.

2 The Purpose of the Migration

Situations which provide examples of race relations arise from migrations and there are certain basic divisions between the kinds of migration, which are sometimes forgotten. Cortes went to Mexico to conquer and convert; a West Indian coming to Britain today comes to earn money in a factory. There is a first basic division between migrants who become the dominant group in the new country, and those who seek only to find a place in a new society, recognizing that at first it will be subordinate.

Where the migrants become the upper group and the natives the lower, there is a division, as I have argued in the last section, between dominant societies and paternalist. In the dominant group again there are differences; in South Africa the line between the upper and lower group is not only rigid—that is, it cannot be passed—but it stays horizontal. A member of the top group must never find himself in a position where he is subordinate to one in the lower. In the Deep South, the line is still rigid but it has tilted to some extent; there are cases of Negroes collecting rent from white tenants. In that transaction, the man from the lower group is on top. In Brazil, which in colonial times must be classed as dominant in relation to the African but paternalist in relation to the Indian, the line eventually both blurred and tilted.

The paternalist or trusteeship relation may also be divided in a variety of ways. Sometimes paternalism turns to dominance; this happened in various Spanish territories in respect of the Indian, for whom Crown protection grew fainter till it disappeared with independence. There was also a basic division between the strictly paternalist British attitude, which was conceived in terms of political devolution and envisaged the son setting up house on his own one day, and the French, conceived in cultural terms, which pictured a day when the son would be so thoroughly assimilated that he might be given a key to the front door of the paternal home, but would not wish to leave. In both cases, there was a tendency to hold on too long, the British prolonging preparations for independence through a period when major decisions were impossible, the French yielding nothing till open conflict developed and the cost of staying grew too high.

Where the migrants were the lower group, there is a division between forced migration and voluntary, with indentured labour in between. The slave societies provide one extreme in the race relations spectrum; not only could a man be sold like a spade or a cart but the slaves lost their language, customs, religion, self-respect. Here was the most extreme form of dominance;* here the symmetry of the classification breaks down, because in the New World both the upper and the lower groups are migrants. Nonetheless, this classification of migrations in respect of the one factor, purpose of the migrant, is useful if only in emphasizing the distinctiveness of the societies to which the lower group came voluntarily and as a minority. They fall into two groups; those, to the United States and Britain, of migrants from under-developed countries seeking higher wages, and those from countries with high skills and a vigorous but too dense a population to countries where skills were less developed—Chinese to Malaya, Sikhs to East Africa, Syrians to West Africa and the Caribbean. The latter group achieved a valuable relationship in a plural society under a strong imperial rule; it may well be called symbiotic, by metaphor with a biological association of plans, in conditions where each can help the other. But their future under national governments is uncertain. In the former group, there is another division; migrants from Europe to the United States and to the United Kingdom have eventually found some means of fitting into the social structure of the nation. This cannot be said with equal conviction of Puerto Ricans or Mexicans in the United States, nor of Sikhs, Pakistanis and West Indians in Britain. It is uncertain whether they are moving towards some kind of integration or towards a subordinate status on the fringe of the main society.

* In the European expansion; I cannot attempt to adjudicate between plantation slavery and the relation of Brahman to out-caste in Southern India. The neighbourhood of an out-caste at many yards distance was polluting to a Brahman.

3 The Nature of the Territory

It is not possible to isolate one factor here so completely as in the case of numerical proportion. The nature of the territory involves the economic attractions it offers to migrants and thus at once brings in the nature of their society; obviously it is only an industrialized people who will be attracted by opportunities of mining for copper or drilling for oil. And the relationship that results from the migration will depend on the demand for labour, the nature of the economy to which the territory is best adapted, the stage of development of the natives, and the ambitions or ideals of the migrants. Nonetheless, the subject has sometimes been discussed as though climate and nature of terrain were the main, if not the sole, determinants.

We are not in this section thinking of the kind of migration in which the migrants expect to be a subordinate minority. Nor need we spend long on the military aspect, though it is obvious that invasions have sometimes been checked by the nature of the country—as the Fulani cavalry were checked by forest in Yorubaland—or have left islands of wild hill country undisturbed and thus created ethnic boundaries, as for example in India, where many pockets of aboriginal tribes were until lately untouched by Hinduism. But let us consider three sets of factors. First, does the territory attract because of its possibilities for trade, for the extraction of minerals, or for agriculture? Secondly, is it tropical or temperate? Thirdly, is it densely or sparsely inhabited?

It is clear that all of these factors are interlocking. Trade is more likely to be profitable if there is a fairly dense population and a dense population inevitably means a developed social system. The migrations primarily interested in trade were Dutch and English and to some extent the Portuguese; they traded to the far East and the West Coast of Africa, all densely populated and tropical countries. Political control was not usually desired and at first was often regarded as a dangerous entanglement, to be avoided if possible. But since goods had to be collected to await the arrival of a ship, a station was necessary, which in a loosely administered country might have to be defended, and so, step by step, a wider political control often seemed increasingly desirable if not inevitable. But the alternative, of trade without political control, always seemed possible; in the case of China, European powers established a string of ports and islands from which to trade; the relinquishment of India was the easier because it was believed that trade with an independent state might be at least as profitable as with a dependency, while the cost of holding down a rebellious dependency might become formidable. If the prime object was trade, the relationship had usually an element of fluidity.

Similar considerations operated in the case of minerals. It was for long satisfactory to obtain copper from Chile and oil from Persia without political control and at the end of the nineteenth century the relations of management with labour were not very different in such territories from those in colonial territories, where the exploiting power had direct political control. Unskilled labour on low wages, skilled supervisory labour from the exploiting country at very high wages, management from the exploiting territories—this three-tier organization was the general rule. Independent countries however began earlier to press for a share in management and sometimes for the training of locals for supervisory and skilled jobs; with colonial countries which achieved independence it became a matter of high priority to substitute for the three-tier racial pattern of employment a continuum in which the natives would play a full part. Only in South Africa and Rhodesia has the colonial pattern of employment been maintained unaltered.

But it is where land has been the main interest of the invading group that race relations have been most affected. This must involve political control. Where the territory was sparsely populated, the previous inhabitants have usually been at a fairly primitive stage of development and have been driven back or exterminated. If the country is tropical—as in Brazil and the Caribbean—they have been replaced by imported labour and the plantation-slave type of economy has grown up. Where the country is temperate—Northern United States, Australia, New Zealand—ranches or wheat farms have been established, intensive of capital rather than labour, or small mixed farms worked by the family. But a question must be asked at this stage of anyone who believes that climate is a main determinant of the economy and therefore of the relationship. Virginia is suited to growing tobacco and cotton—therefore there were plantations and the slave system, and all that follows. This distinguishes Virginia from Massachusetts.

But consider Australia; Victoria and Tasmania are temperate wheat and apple-growing countries not so different from New England. Much of Queensland on the other hand is sugar country; why did no slave economy develop there? The aboriginals, like the American Indians, were driven back; the change in world attitudes had ended the slave trade before Queensland began to be developed, but why were plantations not developed with indentured labour from India, as in Natal, Trinidad, Guyana, Mauritius and Fiji? The answer surely lies not in the climate but in the attitudes of white Australians; they took an important historical decision.

On the other hand, where the native population was dense, it could not be driven back or exterminated. Further, no country will support a dense population unless it is organized in a fairly compact social structure; there are leaders and those who obey. It was usually possible to obtain control of the machinery for government which already existed. In temperate areas such as the hills of Mexico and Peru, the native peasantry was expropriated and eventually became virtually serfs; in parts of Africa, notably Nyasaland and Matabeleland, they fared no better. In tropical areas—notably India—the peasantry simply changed masters; the dues they had previously paid through official fiefholders to the Emperor or to the Raja they now paid to a more impersonal treasury. This was also very much what happened in West Africa, although the system of indirect rule which the British adopted in the twentieth century somewhat obscured what was happening.

Thus the nature of the territory everywhere influenced the relationships that eventually emerged. But it was not the sole determining factor, and must always be considered in relation to the economic interests of the upper group, their political and social ideals and the degree of control exercised by the parent government. Where land was the main interest, a more rigid relationship was liable to arise than in the case of trade or minerals; in temperate countries sparsely inhabited, forms of farming which did not demand much labour were employed and the natives were generally driven out; in tropical countries, they were replaced by slave labour. In countries densely inhabited, the temperate model is the Spanish *hacienda*; the tropical, the British District Officer and the collector of land revenue or hut tax.

4 The Nature of the Conquered People

A broad general rule has already been suggested: when the conquered people were extremely primitive, they were driven out or exterminated, whereas where their society was highly developed, the conquerors simply took over the government. But the fate of the intermediate peoples is various and not easy to explain. Consider the Maoris in comparison with the Bantu-speaking peoples of Southern Africa and the American Indians of the northern plains. The Maoris were a stone age people, hunters and food-gatherers, loosely organized in clans and, by any test except artistry in carving, the most primitive of the three. It is equally clear that their treatment has been more favourable; they have kept, in comparison, a higher proportion of their land, there has been no formal colour bar in schools or employment, they have been represented in Parliament, intermarriage has taken place.

It has already been said that the Maoris were admired for their physical beauty and that the conduct they valued was in many ways similar to that admired by Europeans at earlier stages of their history. But the latter is to some extent true both of Zulus and Redskins, both of whom have been identified with the Noble Savage and made the heroes of popular stories. Umslopogaas,* like the Last of the Mohicans, is a noble figure. Of all three, the conquering whites cherished a double image, one romantic, favourable, and based on conditions that have long ceased, one derogatory and based on observation imperfectly understood. Why then has the difference in treatment been so considerable?

The Maori seem to have been less closely organized into tribal groups than the other two; one writer[53] in fact speaks of the 'granular' nature of their society and says that they were 'anarchically individualist', but he is combating a view previously widespread among Europeans and may slightly over-emphasize. Their basic unit was the *whanau*, the descendants of one man, still living or recently living; such units were linked in the *hapu*—lineage or clan—which had common rights in fishing and hunting areas, but the links grew looser as they rose above the *whanau*. The *hapus* only occasionally formed loose confederations for special purposes. It might be the case that this comparative individualism made them fit more easily into a competitive European type of society.

* Umslopogaas is the native hero of several stories by Rider Haggard.

F

If this were so, however, one might expect to find Europeans in Southern Africa holding in higher repute the less tightly organized groups. But the reverse is the case; whites in Rhodesia, for example, generally speak of the Matabele, who were organized as a primitive state, with more respect than of the various Mashona groups, who, by the time Europeans entered the country, were effectively organized at levels hardly higher than the Maori. In what is now Zambia, the whites reserved any admiration they might express for the warlike Bemba, the Ba-Rotse, the Angoni, not for the Tonga. They could be generous to those, whose virtues were military and who had been defeated. Those incapable of military opposition were at first despised for that simple reason. But they responded more readily than the warriors to missionary enterprise; as they acquired Western education, they became potential rivals and contempt was mingled with resentment.

The conclusion seems inescapable that it is on the side of the upper group that one must look for the main reasons for different treatment. White New Zealanders never had any serious fears of being swamped or overrun. At the time of the Treaty of Waitangi, there was plenty of room for both Maori and Pakeha; by the time of the Maori wars, the Pakehas were firmly on top, with all the resources of the British Empire to call on if need be. Britain, to them, was never a threat, as to the Afrikaners. They could afford to be generous.

The general rule, then, seems to be that while the extremely primitive—Bushmen or Tasmanians—were treated as vermin and the highly developed were ruled as subjects, in the middle band of the spectrum, differences in the customs and stage of development of the defeated were of marginal importance. The sense of security of the conquerors was the overriding factor.

5 Sexual Attitudes

Some stress has been laid in the descriptive sections of the last chapter on sexual attitudes; they are doubly important in race relations, as a distinguishing mark of the kind of relationship that exists, and also as a cause of racial feeling. Where the men of a superior group make free with the women of a socially lower group but jealously guard their own, resentment will obviously be acute among men of the lower group. But the initial shock may be deadened by long and brutal custom. In the Caribbean and the Deep South a stage of degradation was sometimes reached when men regarded the prostitution of their women as a matter for congratulation, this being the way to social progress. Of all the legacies of slaving, this has been psychologically the most far-reaching; for the Negro male, it has meant a second-rate status in the family as well as in society; it lies at the heart of hopelessness in the lower-class Negro and of bitterness in the Negro intellectual.

I have already suggested, in the section on Brazil, that the mere fact of sexual contact does not imply any warmth of feeling; indeed, it may convey a deep contempt for the woman thus used, and may confirm the male of the upper group in the arrogant conviction that he really is, by nature, the superior of the man whose woman he takes. We have also noticed that paternity is acknowledged in some societies but that in others the stain of the mother's status is passed on to the child. These points suggest that we have two different sets of attitudes in a counterpoint; one concerns equality and social stratification, the other concerns attitudes to sex, feelings of guilt, shame or prudery on the one hand, of pride in sexual potency on the other. Among the upper middle classes of Victorian England, feelings about sex which we may inadequately describe as prudery were strong; on the other hand, the society was stratified and the 'premise of inequality' was nervously guarded. The one set of values forbade incontinence outside marriage, the other marriage with anyone but an equal. A hundred years earlier, attitudes in respect both of sex and inequality had been different; both had been taken for granted more readily and in general there had been much less anxiety about sexual contacts outside marriage. The Portuguese showed little anxiety about sex outside marriage, which they did not regard as implying equality; they were firmly hierarchical and therefore confident that free Negroes would stay at the bottom of the social ladder and could thus be freed without danger. But marriage with Negroes, which would imply a formal equality, was practically unknown in colonial times.

To illustrate the counterplay of the two sets of attitudes, it is worth considering four relationships, marriage, concubinage, exploitation, and acknowledgement of paternity. Clearly only marriage recognizes full equality, but there is a world of difference between the kind of friendly long-standing concubinage which has been described in Burma and the brutal exploitation of a Negro woman in the Deep South by a white policeman, whose interest is momentary and purely sexual. And there is clearly a division between societies in which the children belong to the same group as the father and those in which they are relegated to the lowest social group.

The chart which follows, like all such attempts, necessarily simplifies relationships which are much subtler than it can show. Indeed, one of its chief interests is the difficulties of classification which it presents; another is the change which takes place in time.

The classification, I must again emphasize, is necessarily crude. The word 'condoned' means that there is some degree of disapproval but that the practice is widespread and not seriously condemned. The Brahman prohibition was social and religious, not legal, but extremely strong and offspring could not be acknowledged. I find it extremely difficult to include Brazil or Jamaica because there are so many nuances of meaning in the words used. Various studies of Brazil report university students—who are expected to be less conventional than most of the population—expressing themselves overwhelmingly against marriage with a *preto*—a black—but how exactly would they define him? The word really has come to mean 'belonging to the lower classes and looking as though of slave origin'. The table adds force to the distinction between Dominant and Paternal societies, but shows variations within both. It is notable that, in recent years, South Africa is more rigid than the Deep South, though this was not always so. The difference must be due mainly to the insecurity of the Afrikaners, a minority in their own country, threatened by a whole black continent, with no powerful ally that does not express disapproval of their racial policies.

In the paternal type of society there is much less rigidity and great variations in attitude to sexual contact between races. In British society there was obviously a great change in both moral and aesthetic *tone* between the periods of *Tom Jones* and *Tristram Shandy* and the writings of Jane Austen and Thackeray. Sex had become something that could not be mentioned in polite literature or a lady's drawing-room; it had gone underground. At the same time, since the French Revolution, there was a nervousness about equality. Marriage with someone of a markedly lower social status was disgraceful—particularly of a lady with a man of lower status

TABLE 2

*Social Attitudes to Sex and Race: Various societies classified
in respect of four relationships*

Society	Marriage	Concubinage	Exploitation in casual encounter	Classification of children
South Africa, 1968	Forbidden by law	Forbidden by law	Forbidden by law	Lower group
Deep South, 1960	Forbidden by law	Disgrace	Condoned	Lower group
Brahman village, 1910	Forbidden	Forbidden	Forbidden	Lower group
Tutsi, 1960	Disapproved	Accepted	Accepted	Father's group, if married
British India, 1780	Accepted but rare	Accepted but rare	Accepted	Intermediate
British India (Officers, 1880)	Very rare; disgrace	Very rare; kept secret	Rare; secret	Intermediate
British India (Non-commissioned, 1880)	Rare; condoned	Rare; condoned	Accepted	Intermediate
British India, 1947	Accepted	Condemned	Condemned	Follows one parent or other
British Burma, 1880–1940	Accepted	Accepted	Condoned	Intermediate but, if wealthy, follows father
British West Africa, 1955	Accepted (doubtfully)	Condoned	Condemned	Intermediate but, if wealthy, follows father
Mexico (time of Cortes)	Accepted	Accepted	Accepted	Father's group, if known
Mexico (Spanish-Indian), 17th century	Condoned if heiress wealthy	Accepted	Accepted	Intermediate
Mexico, 1950	Accepted	Accepted	Accepted	Upper group
New Zealand	Unwillingly accepted	Disapproved	Disapproved	Follows one parent
Victorian class system	Disgrace	Disapproved (except for aristocrats)	Disapproved	Follows father if acknowledged
Britain, 1968	Disapproved by relatives	Disapproved	Disapproved	Not yet known

—but the aristocracy still retained some memories of the feudal past and a lady's maid might find a way to a competence and an establishment of her own by the same path that brought freedom to a slave woman in the Caribbean. A lord might keep a chorus girl but such behaviour would be shocking to the middle-classes.[54] All this was reflected in attitudes abroad and accounts for the change in British behaviour in India.

Burma and West Africa, in contrast with India, indicate that a permissive attitude to sex on the side of the subordinate group make a difference to the relationship. There are parallels to this in the Pacific. Apart from this, the chart speaks for itself; the points it makes have already been noted in Chapter 7. It serves as a summary and a guide to the multiplicity of situations and relationships.

6 Nature of Dominant Group

In this chapter we have been trying to isolate factors which affect certain relationships and it has not been easy; as we have progressed, each factor has seemed to be linked with others. But the most complex, the least isolable, is the nature of the dominant society.

The lesson of all we have considered so far suggests that, for a true understanding of the relationship between any two peoples who have come together in one state, it is essential to have a sympathetic understanding of *both* the parent societies. The kind of schematic approach with which we have been experimenting cannot do more than suggest some contrasts and lines of enquiry; like the others, it is more useful in a negative sense than a positive, because it does refute certain simple solutions which do not take enough factors into account.

We are still thinking of the situations arising out of the European expansion. There are, I suggest, five main dimensions in which dominant groups have varied. They may be stated crudely as pairs of opposites, between each of which stretches a continuum, so that they are seldom bleak alternatives and there are infinite variations. But in all the relations we have looked at, an element in the result has been the position of the dominant society in these five dimensions. Is the social structure stratified or egalitarian? Is the state autocratic or democratic? Does it centralize power or devolve it? Is it Catholic or Protestant? Are the males proud of their sexual potency or guilt-ridden and secretive? And to these five dimensions might be added rather doubtfully two more, open to objection even more than the others as impressionistic and hard to generalize about: do they pride themselves on their rational powers of logic or on their common-sense in dealing with a situation as it arises? Do they feel that their state must be glorious or do they look on its special virtues as independent of glory? I do not propose to dwell on these last two but they do emphasize a difference between, let us say, the French and the Dutch approaches, which has a bearing.

With several of the five main dimensions, we have dealt to some extent already and we need not dwell on them further. But two general points must be made first; there are clearly links between these dimensions; Spain under Philip II, for example, would answer affirmatively to the first in each pair of questions, the state being stratified, autocratic, centralizing, Catholic, and the males seldom guilt-ridden about their sexuality. But the answers would not in every case be equally consistent; the dimensions may vary independently and they vary at different periods. More importantly, the effect on race relations is often paradoxical; it is certainly not always what would have been expected by nineteenth-century Anglo-Saxon liberals. I have suggested that egalitarianism operated *against* the release of slaves in the Deep South; the autocracy of Philip II was some protection to the American Indians; the British tendency to devolve power had unfortunate results for slaves in the New World and for the Africans of South Africa and Rhodesia.

We have mentioned more than once a dominant society of the ancient world, Sparta. It was an important aspect of the Spartan social structure that the full citizens were *equals*—peers. They were an egalitarian aristocracy—conceding no rights to the Helots, and to the Perioikoi some rights but little esteem. There is a parallel with the Afrikaners, who have separated themselves rigidly from the people who surround them but among themselves are distinctly free from stratification and who would claim that they are democratic. But by this they mean egalitarian among themselves; they would reject a concept of democracy which permitted open and radical criticism of the racial policies of Afrikaner nationalism. The principle enunciated by Jefferson Davis is still valid; the presence of a rigidly defined subordinate group raises all men of the upper group to the same level.

The centralization of power in metropolitan hands operated in favour of the subordinate group in the Spanish Empire, and to some extent in most empires. In British territories in Africa and the Caribbean, this was usually the case, but not always in India, where metropolitan concern for the manufacture of cotton goods in Britain overruled the views of officials in India and committed an injustice which Indian officials sought to avoid. But India is an exception to many generalizations. In general, the metropolitan power did give some protection against exploitation but, by its centralization, frequently drove colonial residents to rebellion. And in Spanish America, in English America, in South Africa, and Rhodesia, the native suffered.

It has been argued, notably by Professor Arnold Toynbee, that for the ruling power to be Catholic rather than Protestant has been of overriding importance in determining the course of race relations. Let it first be said that neither Mexico nor the other Spanish territories nor Brazil is at present so free as he suggests from race consciousness, prejudice, and discrimination. But, of course, he is right in so far that these are countries of fluid definition, with little overt discrimination, and, as I have indicated, I believe that the decision of the Catholic Kings to unify their realms on the basis of Catholicism played an important part in this. On the other hand, French islands in the Caribbean appear to be more rigidly stratified on racial lines than any others. But I do not think that the political decision of Ferdinand and Isabella exhausts the influence of Catholicism. The externalization of conflict by confession and absolution reduces the burden of sinfulness which in many forms of Protestantism can only be removed by the rare phenomenon of total conversion. The insistence that there is no mediator, that there can be help from no friendly, comfortable saints; the emphasis on the gathered community of converted souls as opposed to the universalism of the parish, in which there is room for even the most intermittent believer who has received baptism as an infant—all these Protestant tendencies keep conflict internal and feed that sense of guilt and inadequacy that is so often projected on to another racial group. And, as I suggested earlier, emphasis on predestination for grace or salvation encourages a division of the world on rigid lines into 'us' and 'them'. The virtues specially admired two generations ago in New England and the North of England—sturdy individualism, self-confidence, self-reliance, blunt outspoken honesty—were fostered by the Protestant ethic and tip over easily into an insensitive and even arrogant intolerance. It is a consequence of these deep differences of approach that some Protestant sects have sometimes paid attention to the fiercer and more intolerant passages of the Old Testament about the extirpation of the Canaanites, and have identified themselves with the Jews fresh from the desert. All these influences have been at work in South Africa and in the Deep South.

Neither of these great branches of Christian belief have lived up to their own ideals; both have produced saintly men who fought for what they believed against the currents of power, of economic interest, and of that intense desire to preserve unaltered its identity and its way of life that is common to every human group. In this respect, the Roman Catholic Church has often been found on the side of entrenched privilege, particularly in Latin America. But the Catholic approach to the soul has tended to reduce in men the kinds of passion that arouse the worst racial intolerance.

The atmosphere that results from this has sometimes concealed the facts. The French regard themselves as 'peu raciste' but the ruthlessness with which they suppressed the rebellion of 1947 in Madagascar seems to have involved something more than even the most cynical calculation of political expediency; reports, not yet fully verified, speak of growing resentment in metropolitan France against Algerians. This discrepancy between Brazilian professions and practice in marriage has already been noted. In short, as we consider each of these dimensions, the need to resist any simple or single explanation is reinforced.

9
The Heart of the Matter

LET us come back to the heart of the matter and consider what prospects there are of people of different Biological Race living peacefully side by side in the same nation-state. It is no use considering this in terms of what we should like. We have to recognize that in man's psychological structure there are adverse forces which can easily be roused; further, no state will ever be free from some degree of injustice and some inequality in the distribution of power, wealth, and esteem. Nor have we found any state where there are marked physical differences attributed to race, which are not regarded as to some extent indications of social status. Judgements that they have no social significance are usually superficial. And where there are groups within the state perceived to be different from the majority, the majority's sense of resentment at injustice or inequality will tend to crystallize along the line of difference.

It is an essential part of the argument of this book that what is important is the *perception* of difference. Catholics and Protestants in Northern Ireland; Hindus and Muslims in the Punjab; nobles and serfs in Russia—all have felt themselves to be essentially different from each other. Only occasionally, and as it were with surprise, have they recognized common human qualities. They speak sometimes as though they were divided by race—but it is Notional Race. The conviction that race, in the biological sense, carries with it a difference of this same kind—a difference in essential nature—is a result of the social, political and economic history and structure of the society in which it occurs. Resentment may crystallize along lines of religion or language—of Notional Race as well as Biological—but so long as there are clearly marked differences of physical appearance, these provide an obvious and easy opportunity for deep-rooted passions to express themselves.

There is thus a danger which cannot be wholly avoided; the sensible question to ask is, to what extent it can be reduced. Here there are two paradoxes which must be faced and accepted. Past systems of extremely rigid social stratification, like the classical empires and the slave system in the Deep South, have often appeared tranquil and secure, in spite of great inequality and injustice. This is because the subordinate group sees no escape. But when the dams do break, the results are likely to be cataclysmic. One such cataclysm has recently occurred, in 1960, in Ruanda; here the Tutsi system of dominance was not so extreme as slavery in the Deep South, but when it came to an end, the Hutu reprisals seemed to express four hundred years of resentment. Again, the refugee from a racially rigid society to one rather more fluid often has moments of nostalgia for the past, when he 'knew where he was'. It may be an extremely painful task to live in a society where race is a means of social recognition that is fluidly defined. Nonetheless, anyone who has read this book to this point is likely to judge that it is better to live in a fluid society than a rigid, whatever the cost. Further, in all the fluid societies there is a proclaimed abhorrence of discrimination on grounds of race and this may affect the direction of change.

Let us try to sum up the main points that have emerged from the last three chapters. They are five—the multiplicity of situations that have arisen; the uniqueness of each situation; the inadequacy of any single factor to explain the differences; the element of historical change and of human decision involved in that change; finally, the relation of every situation to the general world-wide revolt against the 'premise of inequality'.

The revolt is against all inequalities of opportunity arising from birth; it is a revolt against privilege of class as well as race. But it has a special bitterness in its racial aspect, which is due not entirely to memories of past injustice. For the majority no doubt it is mainly anger at present exclusion and rejection. But for the more educated, it is the sense of betrayal, of having been excluded from something seen suddenly to be no longer worth having, but for which an older, simpler, and happier—though possibly imaginary

—world has been abandoned. It is the emptiness of being left with nothing to believe in.

Let us consider realistically the dangers. There are those who speak of a world war between rich white nations and poor non-white. This seems unlikely, if the word 'war' is used in the sense of declared and open hostility between states; military power is still overwhelmingly on the side of the rich. But in a world dominated by the rivalry of super powers, minor guerrilla wars on frontiers, deep underlying racial antagonism whipped up with the purpose of healing internal disunion, these indeed seem likely to develop and continue. And they are liable to paralyse international agencies and the growth of international functions which in the long run embody man's hope of survival.

Several factors operate to alienate the poor and non-white nations from the United States and Western Europe; it is no part of the purpose of this book to enumerate them, but high among them is the conviction that the expansion of Europeans in the last two hundred years did them grave damage, spiritual as well as material—and that, within the white states, even today people are treated with indignity on account of their colour. And there can be little doubt that, apart from the international cost, the internal cost of a divided nation is high. There is an economic cost; if there are citizens who are not getting full opportunities of using their ability, skill and talent is being wasted. There is a social cost, in prisons and welfare officers, in remand homes and law courts. There is an educational cost, because where there is no incentive, a hostile spirit to the whole educational system develops. There is a moral cost, of deception and either obsequiousness or aggressive hostility on one side, and on the other, of a callousness which easily grows into brutality and may infect the whole atmosphere with cynicism.

What are the omens? Let us consider, in Britain only, what factors are at work to make relationships more rigid and what are in favour of an easing of the situation. Liable to make things worse in the short run is the general rise in expectations and the widening of circles of comparison; all these induce discontent. As I have insisted throughout this book, the apparent permanence of a situation may make tolerable what would otherwise be utterly intolerable. But in a world of rapid change and rising wages, the slightest inequality is resented, competition is intensified and the temptation is strong to exclude an alien group. Tension would ease again only if progress was far more rapid than seems likely.

Next, in the anonymity of city life, appearance becomes increasingly the only guide to social status. In a community where everyone is known, neither the squire nor the miller need be concerned about being recognized for who they are; everyone knows them and has a shrewd idea of how they will behave. But in the city, a man must *show* who he is, and the most permanent badge is colour; it is therefore likely to be increasingly a mark of identification. There is also the perpetual danger of the unscrupulous politician, who for his personal advantage, or to heal rifts among his followers, will make a scapegoat of any obviously different minority. And this will be the easier because of the pressures of modern life, the nervous tension created by intense competition, the anxieties of a world of social change, of uncertain beliefs and of values which are constantly in question. From this turmoil and insecurity one escape is into violent hostility, but the more common, particularly in England, is withdrawal into a small complacent world, sealed against contact with anything alien.

All this must be seen against the breakdown of the 'premise of inequality' which was once a condition of human progress and which was the cement of English social life. A part of it has been the breaking up of local communities and, in the amorphous undifferentiated society that results, there is a hunger for something smaller and more home-like than the great nation-state. As horizontal class barriers have begun to be eroded, vertical regional barriers begin to go up. It is no longer the high road to success to give up being Welsh; a Welsh-speaking middle class begins to appear, and as in north-western Guatemala, the possibility emerges of a regionalism in which the leaders are truly native. There are signs of it in Brittany, in the Basque Country, in Scotland; how long will it be before it appears in the North Island of New Zealand and, indeed, wherever there is an ethnic minority with a territorial centre?

Regionalism is an omen that, if heeded in good time, need not be frightening. And there are some elements in the British situation that are encouraging. The white British, in the first place, have no need for fear on the scale of the Afrikaner; they may not like foreign cooking-smells or the feeling that their street is coming down in the world, but they are not likely to be outnumbered in the country as a whole. They are in no serious danger and one of their most cherished remaining ideals is fair play. Appeals to this ideal elicit a quite different response from appeals to a sense of national homogeneity. The situation is still fluid; attitudes about colour have not yet hardened into fixed patterns of behaviour and, though this fluidity and uncertainty may cause embarrassment, or even worse, it means that there is still the possibility of leadership.

All that we have seen in other societies confirms the possibility of change and much of it suggests that there is a strong element of what may loosely be called 'decision' in the line that development takes. It is perhaps seldom the conscious decision of a single man who weighs the arguments for and against; rather it is the 'decision' of a society, in which some debate may take place or it may not. But, after hanging on the balance, the situation swings one way or the other. This point has been reached in Britain and vigorous leadership might still swing it towards fluidity. Such leadership would have on its side one powerful asset in youth, which is more tolerant in this respect than middle-age. Further, if we have been right that a stiff Calvinism favours a rigid view of race relations, then the growth of a morality based on personal relations rather than rules seems likely to favour a more fluid attitude.

It has sometimes been assumed that contact between groups divided by race, culture, or religion will in itself bring about better relations. This is by no means necessarily so; it will depend on leadership on both sides and on the circumstances in which people meet. Contact may lead to hostility over some irreconcilable point of prestige, on which both parties become entrenched. It may lead to bored and irritated incomprehension. But thousands can give evidence of getting through the first difficulties and of coming to a knowledge of some person of another race so that, as talk develops, guards are dropped, speech is free, and differences are utterly forgotten. Skin colour becomes an irrelevance; indeed it can be a shock to remember it.

This is personal experience. It is perhaps too much to hope that the behaviour of nations will be based on personal understanding. What has to emerge, indeed is perhaps in the process of emerging, is a new structure, both of national and international society. Stratified hierarchy goes and its place seems likely to be taken by a series of interlocking and overlapping circles of interest which are also systems of esteem and prestige; these will increase as leisure increases and the health of a society will perhaps depend on the extent to which they overlap and to which esteem is not always concentrated on the same person in different contexts. That is to say, national society, instead of being racially homogeneous and stratified by class, is perhaps moving towards a much more plural solution, in which groups based on ethnic, cultural, and leisure interests will increase in number and diversity. Such a development would surely in the long run lead to the strengthening of a new international structure.

On these points it remains for the nation to take a decision. But everyone can help the nation in its decision by finding out something of the way in which majorities and minorities behave towards each other and how Biological Race is regarded in a wide variety of societies. The study of race relations may itself be one factor in the many-stranded web of national decision.

Numbered References

Chapter 1

  1 Robert Bridges: *The Testament of Beauty*, II, 68–70

Chapter 2

  2 J. A. Frazer Roberts: 'A Geneticist's View of Human Variability',
    in *Man, Race and Darwin*
  3 Lee J. Cronbach: *Harvard Educational Review*, Spring 1969
  4 J. A. de Gobineau: *The Inequality of the Human Races* (Quoted
    in Banton: *Race Relations*)
  5 Quoted in Banton: *Race Relations*
  6 E. A. Hooton: *Up from the Ape*
  7 J. A. Fraser Roberts: op. cit.
  8 G. Ainsworth Harrison: 'The Biological Effects of Miscegena-
    tion', in *Man, Race and Darwin*

Chapter 3

  9 Otto Klineberg: *Race Differences*
 10 P. E. Vernon: 'Race and Intelligence', in *Man, Race and Darwin*
 11 T. Dobzhansky: *Genetics and the Origin of Species*
 12 P. E. Vernon: op. cit.
 13 Claude Brown: *Manchild in the Promised Land*
 14 Jessie Bernard: *Marriage and Family among Negroes*

Chapter 4

 15 R. K. Merton: *Social Theory and Social Structure*
 16 E. L. Hartley: *Problems in Prejudice*
 17 See Tolstoy: *Father Sergius*, 'Kasatsky belonged to those men
    who while deliberately . . . condoning impurity in themselves
    required ideal and angelic purity in their women, regarded

all unmarried women of their circle as possessed of such
purity . . .'
18 Gilberto Freyre: *The Masters and the Slaves*
19 Mannoni: *Prospero and Caliban*. Also many novels of Southern
Africa
20 Philip Mason: *The Birth of a Dilemma*
21 Peter Abrahams: *Tell Freedom*
Frantz Fanon: *The wretched of the earth*
James Baldwin: *The fire next time*
Eldridge Cleaver: *Soul on ice*
22 Philip Mason: *Prospero's Magic*
23 Eldred Jones: *Othello's Countryman*
24 Philip Mason: '. . . But Oh my soul is white', in *Encounter*
25 G. K. Hunter: *Othello and Colour Prejudice*
26 H. Wagatsuma: 'The social perception of skin colour in Japan',
in *Daedalus*

Chapter 5

27 J. J. Maquet: *The Premise of Inequality in Ruanda*

Chapter 6

28 M. Banton: *Race relations*
29 R. Heber: *Indian Journal*
30 J. S. Furnivall: *Netherlands
India: a study of plural economy*
31 Morse Stephens: *Albuquerque*. Oxford 1892
32 J. A. Pitt-Rivers: *After the Empire*
33 Philip Woodruff (pseud.): *The men who ruled India*, Vol. 1

Chapter 7

34 I. D. MacCrone: *Race attitudes in South Africa*
35 (sic) South Africa Bureau of Racial Affairs: *Integration or
Separate Development*
36 South Africa. Commission for the Socio-Economic Development
of the Bantu Areas. *Report* (The Tomlinson Report)
37 Klein: *Slavery in the Americas*
38 Quoted in Banton: *Race relations*
39 Klein: ibid
40 See Mason: *The birth of a dilemma*
41 S. de Madariaga: *Spain*
42 Jose Matos Mar: *Ethnic discrepancies and social change in the
Andean Region*. Unpublished paper read at Chatham House
(1965)

See also: Philip Mason: 'Gradualism in Peru', in *Race*, Vol. 8, No. 1, July 1966

43 P. L. Doughty: *Peruvian Highlanders in a changing world*: social integration and culture change in an Andean district. Unpublished PhD thesis, Cornell University, 1963

44 C. Prado: *The colonial background of modern Brazil*

45 Henry Coor, 1790–91, quoted in David Lowenthal: *Caribbean Societies*

46 Frantz Fanon quoted in Lowenthal: *Caribbean Societies*

47 Soyinka, Wole, quoted in Lowenthal: *Caribbean Societies*

48 J. Harre: *Maori and Pakeha: a study of mixed marriages in New Zealand*

49 G. O. Trevelyan: 'The Competition-wallah' in *Macmillan's Magazine*, 1864

50 Paul Foot: *Immigration and Race in British Politics*

Chapter 8

51 J. M. Steward: *Contemporary change in traditional societies*, Vol. 1

52 M. Harris: *Patterns of Race in the Americas*

53 J. E. Ritchie: *The making of a Maori*

54 Victorian novels are full of veiled references on the theme of the squire's son and the dairy maid. Surtees is a useful source for information about life in rural England; the hero of *Ask Mamma* is the son of a lady's-maid, hastily married off and supplied with a dowry by a noble admirer. See also the popular drama *Maria Marten: or the Murder in the Red Barn*, which was played by touring companies throughout the nineteenth century. And see in the reading-list Cuminos on Victorian Sexual Respectability

Select Bibliography

FOR most of the chapters, there is a short reading list.

Chapter 1

I have referred in this chapter to Huxley: *Evolutionary Ethics*, which is important for the basic assumptions. Huxley's account of the 'how' of evolution is illuminating and most valuable but his insistence that it is all due to blind chance seems to me dogmatic and doctrinaire and I am quite unconvinced, as I argued at length in *Christianity and Race*.

At an early stage, anyone proposing to continue with this subject should read, as an antidote to my views:

BANTON, M.: *Race Relations*, London, Tavistock, 1967

VAN DEN BERGHE, P. L.: *Race and Racism*, New York, Wiley, 1967

Chapter 2

Two sources include a number of important papers:

Man, Race and Darwin, published for the Royal Anthropological Institute and the Institute of Race Relations by OUP, London, 1960

Harvard Educational Review, Vol. 39, 1969. No. 1 contains an article by A. Jensen 'How Much Can we Boost IQ and Scholastic Achievement?', which was answered by, among others, J. S. Kagan and Ltt J. Cronbach in No. 2. Jensen has replied in No. 3.

BARNICOT, N. A.: 'Biology and Human Variation', in *Race*, May 1960

BARNICOT, N. A.: 'From Darwin to Mendel', in *Man, Race and Darwin*

BARZUN, J.: *Race: a Study in Superstition*, New York, Harper, 1965, Rev. edn

CAIN, A. J.: *Animal Species and their Evolution*, Hutchinson University Library, London 1954

DOBZHANSKY, T.: *Genetics and the Origin of Species*, Columbia University Press, 3rd ed, New York 1951

DUNN, L. C.: *Race and Biology*, Paris, UNESCO, 1951

Gobineau, J. A. de: *Essay on the Inequality of the Human Races*, Heinemann, London, 1915 (Paris, 1853–4)

Harrison, G. A.: 'The Biological Effects of Miscegenation', in *Man, Race and Darwin*

Hooton, E. A.: *Up from the Ape*, New York, Macmillan, 1956, Rev. edn

Klineberg, O.: *Race Differences*, New York, Harper, 1935

Morant, G. M.: 'The Significance of Racial Differences', in *The Race Question in Modern Science*, Paris, UNESCO, 1956

Roberts, F.: *An Introduction to Human Blood Groups*, London, Heinemann, 1960

Roberts, J. A. Fraser: 'A Geneticist's View of Human Variability', in *Man, Race and Darwin*

UNESCO: *Statement on Race and Racial Prejudice*, Paris, UNESCO, September, 1967

Chapter 3

Biesheuvel, S.: 'African Intelligence: Psychological Tests and their Application to Non-European Peoples', in *Yearbook of Education*, London, Evans, 1949

Brown, C.: *Manchild in the Promised Land*, New York, Macmillan, 1965

Dobzhansky, T.: *Genetics and the Origin of Species*, see Chapter 2, above

Harvard Educational Review, Vol 39, 1969 (see Chapter 2, above)

Hebb, D. O.: *The Organization of Behaviour*, New York, Wiley, 1949

Klineberg, O.: *Race Differences*, see Chapter 2, above

Lee, E. S.: 'Negro Intelligence and Selective Migration, a Philadelphia Test of the Klineberg Hypothesis', in *American Sociological Review*, Vol. 16, 1951

Shuey, A. M.: *The Testing of Negro Intelligence*, Britons Publishing Co., Devon, 1958

Vernon, P. E.: *Intelligence and Cultural Environment*, Methuen, 1969

Vernon, P. E.: 'Race and Intelligence', in *Man, Race and Darwin*

Chapter 4

Abrahams, P.: *Tell Freedom*, London, Faber, 1954

Adorno, T. W. and others: *The Authoritarian Personality*, New York, Harper, 1950

Baldwin, J.: *The Fire Next Time*, New York, Dial Press, 1963

Bethelheim, E. and Janowitz, M.: *Dynamics of Prejudice*, American Jewish Committee, 1950

Bronowski, J.: *The Face of Violence*, Bermerles, 1967

Cleaver, E.: *Soul on Ice*, London, Jonathan Cape, 1969

Fanon, F.: *The Wretched of the Earth*, London, MacGibbon and Kee 1965

Freyre, G.: *The Masters and the Slaves*, see Chapter 7, Section 4, below

HARTLEY, E. L.: *Problems in Prejudice*, New York, King's Crown, 1946

HUNTER, G. K.: *Othello and Colour Prejudice*, Proceedings of the British Academy, Vol. 53, London, O.U.P., 1967

ISAACS, H.: *Scratches on our Minds: American Images of China and India*, New York, Day, 1958

JAHODA, M.: *Race Relations and Mental Health*, Paris, UNESCO, 1960

JONES, E.: *Othello's Countryman*, London, O.U.P., 1965

MANNONI, O.: *Prospero and Caliban: the Psychology of Colonization*, London, Methuen, 1956

MAQUET, J. J.: *The Premise of Inequality in Ruanda*, O.U.P., 1961

MASON, P.: *The Birth of a Dilemma*, London, O.U.P., 1958

MASON, P.: ' ". . . But O My Soul is White": on the Confusion of Biological Accident and Symbolic Metaphor', in *Encounter*, Vol. 30, No. 4, 1968

MASON, P.: *Prospero's Magic*, London, O.U.P., 1962

MERTON, R. K.: *Social Theory and Social Structure*, Illinois, Free Press, 1949

ROSE, A. M.: *The Roots of Prejudice*, Paris, UNESCO, 1951

STAFFORD-CLARK, D.: *The Psychology of Persecution and Prejudice*, Council for Christians and Jews, 1960

WAGATSUMA, H.: 'The Social Perception of Skin Colour in Japan', in *Daedalus*, Spring 1967

WRIGHT, R.: *Black Boy*, New York, World, 1950

Chapter 5

BAUDIN, L.: *Daily Life in Peru*, London, Allen and Unwin, 1961

BUSHNELL, G. S.: *Peru*, London, Thames and Hudson, 1963

CHILDE, V. G.: *What Happened in History*, Harmondsworth, Penguin, 1951

GLUCKMAN, M. and COLSON, E., eds: *Seven Tribes of British Central Africa*, London, O.U.P., 1951

HUGHES, A. J. B.: *Kin, Caste and Nation among the Rhodesian Ndebele*, Manchester University Press, 1956

McCULLOCH, M.: *The South Lunda and Related Peoples*, International African Institute, 1951

MAQUET, J. J.: *The Premise of Inequality in Ruanda*, London, O.U.P., 1961

MASON, J. A.: *The Ancient Civilizations of Peru*, Harmondsworth, Penguin, 1957

PRESCOTT, W. H.: *History of the Conquest of Mexico*, University of Chicago Press, 1966

PRESCOTT, W. H.: *History of the Conquest of Peru*, London, Allen and Unwin, 1959

SOUSTELLE, J.: *Daily Life of the Aztecs*, Harmondsworth, Penguin, 1961

VAILLANT, G. C.: *Aztecs of Mexico*, Harmondsworth, Penguin, 1965

WOLF, E. K.: *Sons of the Shaking Earth*, University of Chicago Press, 1959

Chapter 6

BALDWIN, J.: *Notes of a Native Son* (belles lettres), London, Micheal Joseph, 1964

BANTON, M.: *Race Relations*, see Chapter 1, above

BOXER, C. R.: *Race Relations in the Portuguese Colonial Empire, 1415–1825*, Oxford, Clarendon Press, 1963

FANON, F.: *The Wretched of the Earth*, see Chapter 4 above.

FURNIVALL, J. S.: *Netherlands India: a study of plural economy*, Cambridge, C.U.P., 1939

HEBER, R.: *Indian Journal*, London, 1923

KIERNAN, V. G.: *The Lords of Human Kind*, London, Weidenfeld and Nicolson, 1969

MASON, P.: The Revolt against Western Values, in *Daedalus*, Vol. 96, No. 2, 1967

MASON, P.: ' ". . . but O, My Soul is White': on the Confusion of Biological Accident and Symbolic Metaphor', see Chapter 4, above

PITT-RIVERS, J. A.: *After the Empire: Race and Society in Middle America and the Andes*, O.U.P., forthcoming

PRESCOTT, W. H.: *The History of the Conquest of Mexico*, see Chapter 5, above

SEGAL, R.: *Race War*, London, Jonathan Cape, 1966

WOLF, E. R.: *Sons of the Shaking Earth*, see Chapter 5, above

WOODRUFF, P. (pseud.): *The Men who Ruled India* (2 vols.), London, Jonathan Cape, 1953–4

Chapter 7

Section 1

ABRAHAMS, P.: *Tell Freedom*, see Chapter 4, above

HANCOCK, SIR W. K.: *Survey of British Commonwealth Affairs*, London, O.U.P. for Royal Institute of International Affairs, 1942

MacCRONE, I. D.: *Race Attitudes in South Africa: Historical, Experimental and Psychological Studies*, Johannesburg, Witwatersrand University Press, 1937

McMILLAN, W. M.: *Bantu, Boer and Briton: the Making of the South African Native Problem*, Rev. edn, Oxford, Clarendon Press, 1963

MARAIS, J. S.: *The Cape Coloured People 1642–1937*, Johannesburg, Witwatersrand University Press, 1957

MARQUARD, L.: *The Peoples and Policies of South Africa*, 2nd edn, London, O.U.P., 1960

MASON, P.: *An Essay on Racial Tension*, London, O.U.P., 1954

PATTERSON, S.: *Colour and Culture in South Africa*, London, Routledge and Kegan Paul, 1953

SOUTH AFRICA. *Commission for the Socio-Economic Development of the Bantu Areas . . . Report*, Pretoria, Government Printer, 1956 (Chairman: F. R. Tomlinson)

SOUTH AFRICAN BUREAU OF RACIAL AFFAIRS: *Integration or Separate Development*, Stellenbosch, S.A.B.R.A., 1952

VAN DER HORST, S.: 'The Effects of Industrialisation on Race Relations in South Africa', in Hunter, Guy (ed.): *Industrialisation and Race Relations*, London, O.U.P. for Institute of Race Relations, 1965

Section 2

CASH, W. J.: *The Mind of the South*, New York, Knopf, 1941

DOLLARD, J.: *Caste and Class in a Southern Town*, 2nd edn, New York, Harper, 1949

FAULKNER, W.: *Intruder in the Dust* (a novel), Harmondsworth, Penguin, 1966

FAULKNER, W.: *Light in August* (a novel), Harmondsworth, Penguin, 1968

MYRDAL, G.: *An American Dilemma*, New York, Harper, 1944

SMITH, L.: *Killing of the Dream*, New York, Norton, 1949

VANN WOODWARD, C.: *The Strange Career of Jim Crow*, New York, O.U.P., 1955

Section 3

HANKE, L.: *Aristotle and the American Indians*, London, Hollis & Carter, 1959

KLEIN, H. S.: *Slavery in the Americas:* a Comparative Study of Virginia and Cuba, London, O.U.P. for Institute of Race Relations, 1967

MADARIAGA, S. DE: *Spain*, Rev. edn, London, Jonathan Cape, 1961

PAZ, O.: *The Labyrinth of Solitude: Life and Thought in Mexico*, London, Allen Lane, 1967

PITT-RIVERS, J. A.: *After the Empire: Race and Society in Middle America and the Andes*, O.U.P., forthcoming

TANNENBAUM, F.: *Slave and Citizen*, New York, Knopf, 1947

TUMIN, M. M.: *Caste in a Peasant Society*, Princeton University Press, 1952

Section 4

BOXER, C. R.: *Race Relations in the Portuguese Colonial Empire, 1415–1825*, Oxford, Clarendon Press, 1963

FERNANDES, F.: The Weight of the Past, in *Daedalus*, Spring 1967

FREYRE, G.: *The Mansions and the Shanties: the Making of Modern Brazil*, London, Weidenfeld and Nicolson, 1963

FREYRE, G.: *The Masters and the Slaves: a Study in the Development of Brazilian Civilisation*, New York, Knopf, 1946

HARRIS, M.: *Patterns of Race in the Americas*, New York, Walker and Co., 1964

PIERSON, D.: *Negroes in Brazil: a Study of Race Contact at Bahia*, New York, Feffer and Simons, 1967

PRADO, C.: *The Colonial Background of Modern Brazil*, Berkeley, University of California Press, 1967

RODRIGUES, J. H.: *Brazil and Africa*, 2nd edn, Berkeley, University of California Press, 1965

WAGLEY, C. (ed.): *Race and Class in Rural Brazil*, Paris, UNESCO, 1952

Section 5

BRAITHWAITE, L.: Social Stratification in Trinidad, in *Social and Economic Studies*, Vol. 2, Nos. 2–3, 1953

CLARKE, E.: *My mother who fathered me*, London, George Allen and Unwin, 1957

FERMOR, P. L.: *The Traveller's Tree: a Journey Through the Caribbean Islands*, London, Murray, 1965

GOVEIA, E. V.: *Slave Society in the British Leeward Islands at the end of the Eighteenth Century*, New Haven, Yale University Press, 1965

HARLOW, V. T.: *A History of Barbados, 1625–1685*, Oxford, Clarendon Press, 1926

HENRIQUES, F.: *Family and Colour in Jamaica*, London, Eyre and Spottiswoode, 1953

KERR, M.: *Personality and Conflict in Jamaica*, London, Collins, 1963

LAMMING, G.: *In the Castle of My Skin* (a novel), London, Michael Joseph, 1953

LEWIS, G. K.: *The Growth of the Modern West Indies*, London, McGibbon and Kee, 1968

LOWENTHAL, D.: *Caribbean Societies*, London, O.U.P. for Institute of Race Relations, forthcoming

NAIPAUL, V. S.: *A House for Mr. Biswas* (a novel), London, Andre Deutsch, 1961

NAIPAUL, V. S.: *Miguel Street* (a novel), London, Andre Deutsch, 1959

NAIPAUL, V. S.: *The Suffrage of Elvira* (a novel), London, Andre Deutsch, 1948

OLIVIER, S.: *Jamaica, The Blessed Island*, London, Faber, 1936

SALKEY, A. (ed.): *Stories from the Caribbean: an Anthology*, London, Elek Books, 1965

SELVON, S.: *I Hear Thunder* (a novel), London, McGibbon and Kee, 1963

SELVON, S.: *Turn again Tiger* (a novel), London, McGibbon and Kee, 1958

Section 6

FIRTH, R.: *Economics of the New Zealand Maori*, 2nd edn, Wellington, N.Z., R. E. Owen, 1959

*FORSTER, E. M.: *Passage to India*, London, Arnold, 1924

HARRE, J.: *Maori and Pakeha: a Study of Mixed Marriages in New Zealand*, London, Pall Mall Press for Institute of Race Relations, 1966

HARRIS, M.: *Patterns of Race in the Americas*, see Section 4, above

RITCHIE, J. E.: *The Making of a Maori: a Case Study of Changing Community*, Wellington, A. H. and A. W. Read, 1963

RITCHIE, J. E. (ed.): *Race Relations: six New Zealand Studies*, Wellington, Victoria University, 1964

SINCLAIR, K.: *A History of New Zealand*, London, O.U.P., 1961

SORRENSON, M. P. K.: *Maori and European since 1870*, London, Heinemann, 1967

SPEAR, P. (ed.): *The Oxford History of India*, 3rd edn (Pt. 1, rev. by Sir Mortimer Wheeler and A. L. Basham), London, O.U.P., 1967

STEWARD, J. M. (ed.): *Contemporary Change in Traditional Societies*, 3 vols., Chicago, University of Illinois Press, 1957

WOODRUFF, P. (pseud.): *The Men Who Ruled India*, see Chapter 6, above

Section 7

FOOT, P.: *Immigration and Race in British Politics*, Harmondsworth, Penguin, 1965

MASON, P.: 'A Democratic Dilemma: Consensus and Leadership', in *Race*, Vol. 10, No. 4, April 1969

* I have included *Passage to India* because there is much in it that is revealing. It has, however, always seemed to me a highly subjective impression and, though some of the insights into individual minds are sensitive and brilliant, the conclusions about the possibility of understanding between peoples of different culture seem to me far too pessimistic. The frame of mind of the English depicted in this book was not one that I ever encountered, admittedly in another part of India and five years later. Much of the procedure in the court case is illegal.

Rose, E. J. B. and others: *Colour and Citizenship: a Report on British Race Relations*, London, O.U.P., 1969

Chapter 8

Bailey, F. G.: *Tribe, Caste and Nation*, Manchester University Press, 1960

Beteilee, A.: *Caste, Class and Power*, Berkeley and Los Angeles, University of California Press, 1965

Cuminos, P. T.: 'Late Victorian Sexual Respectability and the Social System', in *The International Review of Social History*, Vol. VIII, pts. 1 and 2, 1963

Hutton, J. H.: *Caste in India*, 3rd edn, London, O.U.P., 1961

Isaacs, H.: *India's Ex-Untouchables*, New York, John Day, 1964

Lewis, O.: 'Peasant Culture in India and Mexico', in Marriott, M. (ed.): *Village India*

Marriott, M. (ed.): *Village India*, University of Chicago Press, 1955

Mason, P. (ed.): *India and Ceylon: Unity and Diversity*, London, O.U.P. for Institute of Race Relation, 1967

Index